HELPING YOUR CHILDREN WALK WITH GOD

HELPING YOUR CHILDREN WALK WITH GOD

Phil Phillips
with his father, Syvelle Phillips

THOMAS NELSON PUBLISHERS
Nashville

Published in Nashville, Tennessee, by Oliver-Nelson Books, a division of Thomas Nelson, Inc., Publishers, and distributed in Canada by Lawson Falle, Ltd., Cambridge, Ontario.

The Bible version used in this publication is THE NEW KING JAMES VERSION. Copyright © 1979, 1980, 1982, Thomas Nelson, Inc., Publishers.

Printed in the United States of America.

Library of Congress Cataloging-in-Publication Data

Phillips, Phil.
    Helping your children walk with God / Phil Phillips with Syvelle Phillips.
        p.   cm.
    ISBN 0-8407-9138-0 (pbk.)
    1. Child rearing—Religious aspects—Christianity.
2. Children—Religious life. I. Phillips, Syvelle.
II. Title.
BV4529.P45   1992
248.8′45—dc20   92-31415
                                                          CIP

1 2 3 4 5 6 — 97 96 95 94 93 92

TO
my parents and parents-in-law

Syvelle and Lovie Phillips
and
Gene and Rosetta Calvert

Thank you for passing your faith
to the next generation
and for helping Cynthia and
me to establish
our home on a firm foundation.

To schedule Phil Phillips for interviews and speaking engagements, write to:

Child Affects
P.O. Box 68
Rockwall, TX 75087

Telephone: 214-771-9393
Fax: 214-722-1721

CONTENTS

Foreword   **ix**

1. Confronting the True Attack Against Your Children   **1**

2. Seeing Your Children with God's Eyes   **5**

3. Seeing Your Household as Belonging to the Lord   **26**

4. Embracing What God Requires of You as a Parent   **52**

5. Displaying God's Nature to Your Children   **79**

6. Training Up Your Children Through Simulations   **97**

7. Training Up Your Children Through Discipline and Practice   **124**

8. Sharing God's Word with Your Children   **144**

9. Finding a Church that Puts Your Children First   **176**

10. Keeping the Message Consistent   **215**

11. Facing Your Family's Future with Hope   **234**

12. How Will You Choose?   **257**
Parent's Pledge   **261**

FOREWORD

God has given our son Phil Phillips an amazing love for children. This special love has become a dominant force in Phil's life and ministry. As you read this book you will gain many helpful insights and new understanding that will enrich your life and enhance your ministry to your own offspring. Generations yet to be born will be blessed and some of their eternal destinies changed as you embrace the truths that God is sharing with you through the ministry of our firstborn.

When my wife, Lovie, and I first read the manuscript that is now the book you are holding in your hands, we were very proud parents and pleased that God would call our own flesh and blood to such a unique ministry for this generation of parents and grandparents.

Our second reaction to what Phil wrote, especially in the first chapters, was a deep concern that the truths Phil shared and the issues he addressed so forcefully not be misunderstood. Please read this book in its entirety. You will do yourself and your family a great disservice if you do not prayerfully consider every truth and insight shared on these pages. Be assured that Phil wholeheartedly believes each child must be born again. There is no other way. Every person, child or adult, must come to a saving knowledge of Christ for him- or herself.

Throughout this book, parents are encouraged to expect each child to make a personal, informed choice to serve

God and to experience absolute assurance of salvation that a personal faith in Jesus as Savior brings.

We asked ourselves how Phil came to the understanding that every child born into a Christian family has a special place in the heart of God and that grace and spiritual privilege is always bestowed upon each member of the family who has made Jesus the Lord of their household. And we remember with great joy that, while we did not have the clear insight into the great truths with which Phil so ably speaks and writes today, in our own way, Lovie and I welcomed Phil into our lives and home as an answer to prayer and as a special gift from God. Lovie and I had been married ten years when Phil was born and seventeen years, when a second son, Darin, was born. No words can adequately describe the blessings our sons have been to us. From the day we knew God was going to give us children until this day, we have always understood that our sons belonged to God. We have always thought of them as children of God.

The most natural thing for us to do as parents was to encourage our sons to share our spiritual heritage and our ministry. While we knew the time would come when they would need to say yes to God and His will for their lives, we also knew they would have the right to say no to the claims of Christ and the call of the Holy Spirit. But we never considered that our boys would say no to the Jesus we love so much. We lived in full faith that God would honor His covenant and promises. We knew our sons would make a God-honoring choice for their lives in due time.

By God's grace we did everything within our ability to make it natural and easy for every member of our family to serve God as the best way of life. From the first day our sons received the gift of life, therefore, they were included in our lives in every possible way. Being a Christian family was and is a way of life for the Phillips's home. We worshiped together, prayed for one another, and talked about God—who He is and what He does in our lives. Jesus was a very real and personal friend. Our lives revolved around the church and serving God. *I* was not the pastor, but our *family* provided spiritual leadership and ministry for the congregation we served. It has never been my ministry or Lovie's ministry. It has always been our ministry. Our desire has been to honor every member of our family as equal members of the ministry team.

God's Word, Bible stories, songs, and even games that contributed to our family's spiritual health always had a special place in our home. As God gave us grace, we always lived a Christian life-style. We simply walked in the understanding the Holy Spirit gave us.

Over the years our understanding and wisdom increased. God gave us additional revelation and insights. Lovie and I are the first to confess we made far too many mistakes in our efforts to be good parents. God used even our mistakes and failures to teach us many wonderful lessons. We came to the realization that God will forgive all the mistakes we make and the failures we experience in our efforts to provide spiritual leadership for our family.

We also learned that children will readily forgive fathers and mothers who allow God to give them the grace and humility to apologize to members of the family they have sinned against or failed. Please allow your children to forgive you and set you free from the bondage of guilt. There is a special weight of guilt that is ours to bear when we know that we have failed our own children. Only our children can lift that burden and shame as they forgive us.

I do assure you that children are quick and willing to forgive. Please do not hesitate should you need to ask your children for forgiveness. Be open and to the point. Just ask in your own way to be forgiven. As God forgives and our children forgive, we must allow the Holy Spirit to enable us to forgive ourselves of real or imagined sins against our family. It is never too late. Our losses can be recovered. God will always give us a second chance.

You can provide the spiritual leadership and, with God's help, you will be able to create the climate where your young can be nurtured and developed into strong, mature Christians who will pass on their faith to the next generation.

We feel God has helped Phil, in a special way, to write about what he experienced as he grew up in a home where God was honored and children were valued as special gifts from God. Our children always understood they had been given back to God in total dedication at a very early age.

As you read this book, ask God to give you a new dimension of love for your children. May this special, God-given concern move you to accept the privilege of helping your children find their place in the family of God. May God grant that your descendants bring you the joy and the sense of fulfillment that our sons, Phil and Darin, and their families continue to bring to our lives. The lives our boys live, by the grace of God, does more to authenticate the ministry God has called us to than all the sermons I ever preached or the missionary work we ever undertook. God desires to make our children and their children the crowning achievement of our lives.

H. Syvelle Phillips

1

Confronting the True Attack Against Your Children

Then they also brought infants to Him that He might touch them; but when His disciples saw it, they rebuked them.

But Jesus called them to Him and said, "Let the little children come to Me, and do not forbid them; for of such is the kingdom of God. Assuredly, I say to you, whoever does not receive the kingdom of God as a little child will by no means enter it."

—Luke 18:15–17

The enemy has launched a major, pervasive, all-out attack against our children—one that is insidious, subtle and, for the most part, undetected. It is this: the relegation of our children to second-class spiritual citizenship.

The number one tactic of the enemy against our children is *not* drugs.

It is *not* rock and roll music, rap, hip-hop, or heavy metal.

It is *not* violent, occultic, or sexually titillating television programs, video games, or movies.

It is *not* abortion.

It is *not* pornography.

It is *not* homosexuality.

It is *not* the spirit of divorce that permeates our society.

The number one attack of the enemy today against our children is *an attitude within the church that regards children as second-class spiritual citizens.*

Why do I believe this is the number one attack on our children?

Because if this problem did not exist, all of the other things that we point to and say, *"That* is destroying our children," would not exist—at least not in the form we experience them today.

I firmly believe that the enemy has refined this tactic over the centuries, and that it has begun to emerge with full-blown strength in our churches in the last two or three decades.

The tactic is essentially this:

If the enemy can convince us as Christian adults that our children are not yet ready for Jesus Christ or are too immature to experience the power and presence of the Holy Spirit or are too young to follow the commandments of the Lord God . . .

Then, we will not expose our children to the spiritual experiences that will cause them to grow and develop spiritually into full-grown warriors for the faith.

If the enemy can convince us as Christian parents that our children are somewhat "on hold" with regard to the Lord until they pray a salvation prayer, have a born-again experience, make a full confirmation statement, or join the church . . .

Then, we as Christian parents will avoid—in our attitude as well as our behavior—including our children as equal partners in ministry before the Lord. We, too, will "wait" for them to be initiated, in some way, to the ranks of full Christian membership before we expect and encourage our children to enter into evangelism, the fullness of ministry gifts, or a truly righteous walk with the Lord.

What happens if we yield to the enemy's tactic?

We neglect a significant part of the spiritual development of our children in the home, expecting it to happen elsewhere and at a later date.

We provide alternative programs for our children within the church or at home. We hire baby-sitters for our children while we go away to Christian conferences or special church services. We put our children into the care of a church children's program and entertain them downstairs while parents are upstairs worshiping God and becoming equipped to be His people on this earth.

While we are waiting for our children to grow up and have a salvation experience, they are indeed growing up waiting for us to model spiritual behavior for them, to include them in the practices of the church, and to recognize them as spiritual beings.

Disillusioned and alienated, our children leave the church. They look for spiritual nurture and power outside the church walls. And believe me, the world that the enemy has created offers a great many enticing "spiritual" and "powerful" alternatives to the genuine life-transforming power of almighty God. At the very heart of satanism and occult groups is the promise of spiritual experience and power—a counterfeit, to be sure, but also more experience and power than many of these children have been allowed to or encouraged to experience in a church setting.

And so, our children drift away in droves. More than half of all children in most denominations will exit the church door some time during their teenage years, and many will never return.

While we Christian adults ardently support the call to send out missionaries, evangelists, and outreach teams to win lost souls on distant continents . . .

While we pray and intercede for the lost on faraway shores and behind philosophical curtains . . .

While we support efforts to send literature and media

programs into areas newly opened to the gospel message . . .

Our own children are languishing on the vine and drifting away. We are experiencing a hemorrhage out the back door of the church, even as we attempt to woo distant converts through the front door.

The net result is that the devil saps the life's blood of a church by destroying its most tender members.

Please recognize that this conclusion is not drawn as an attack against the church. I deeply love the church. I believe strongly that the church should truly *be* the church for our children. I have not come to this conclusion quickly or angrily. I weep over this conclusion. It saddens and grieves my soul. Nevertheless, I cannot escape what the Spirit of God has quickened to my heart with such deep conviction.

As I discuss this conclusion with you, I hope you will ponder the way it relates to your own life and church and open yourself to the ministry of the Holy Spirit in your heart. If these words are truly from the Lord, you will sense *His* convicting power and presence. If these words are truth, you will also have a hunger and desire as a Christian parent to begin to see your children more clearly as the Lord sees them. You will seek to establish a strong spiritual environment in your home, one that includes your children as the primary focus of your spiritual mission on this earth. You will have a deep and growing desire to see your church develop programs specifically for the spiritual equipping of your children.

Oh, I pray it may be so!

2

Seeing Your Children
with God's Eyes

Behold, I will send you Elijah the prophet
Before the coming of the great
*   and dreadful day of the LORD.*
And he will turn
The hearts of the fathers to the children,
And the hearts of the children to their fathers,
Lest I come and strike the earth with a curse.
*   —Malachi 4:5–6*

If we truly saw our children the way God sees them, the message of this book would not be necessary.

The fact is . . .

Most of us do *not* see our children as God sees them. We do not see the potential the Lord sees. We do not consider our children to be capable of having the spiritual experiences or of exhibiting the spiritual prowess that He desires to give them and see in them. We do not expect our children to live the renewed, holy lives that God has ordained for them through His covenants.

The fact also is . . .

Children are given high priority in the Scriptures. Proverbs 17:6 asserts, "Children's children are the crown of old men." Psalm 127:3–5 proclaims,

Behold, children are a heritage from the LORD,
The fruit of the womb is a reward.
Like arrows in the hand of a warrior,
So are the children of one's youth.
Happy is the man who has his quiver full of them.

The fact of God's Word is . . .

God desires to have a full, deep, and meaningful relationship with your children.

Your children can have fellowship with God.

Your children can be anointed by God.

Your children can be ordained by God with a special purpose and call on their lives—*as children.*

One of the most famous children's stories in the Bible involves Samuel, who heard the Lord call to him in the night.

Samuel had been born as the result of a prayer by Hannah, who was desperate to have a child. Even before Samuel was conceived, she had dedicated him to the service of the Lord: "O LORD of hosts, if You will indeed look on the affliction of Your maidservant and remember me, and not forget Your maidservant, but will give Your maidservant a male child, then I will give him to the LORD all the days of his life" (1 Sam. 1:11).

When Samuel was weaned, probably between the ages of two and three years, Hannah took him to the house of the Lord along with an offering. The Scriptures say simply, "And the child was young" (1 Sam. 1:24). She said to Eli, the chief priest, "For this child I prayed, and the LORD has granted me my petition which I asked of Him. Therefore I also have lent him to the LORD; as long as he lives he shall be lent to the LORD" (vv. 27–28).

What a wonderful example Hannah is to all of us! She did not consider her son to be her child. Even before his birth, she considered her son to be the Lord's child.

The Scriptures go on to say that "the child ministered

to the LORD before Eli the priest," and "Samuel ministered before the LORD, even as a child, wearing a linen ephod" (1 Sam. 2:11, 18).

The Bible does not say that Samuel was learning to minister or that he was pretending to minister. It says that he was actually doing the ministry of a priest *as a child!*

Let me share with you at the outset of this book four principles on which I stake my life, my children's lives, and my ministry.

Principle 1:
Your Children Are the Lord's . . . NOW

The general prevailing outlook in most Protestant evangelical and charismatic churches in which I have spoken or visited seems to be this: We must get our children "saved." The premise is that our children are on the outside, deep in sin, and in need of divine deliverance. We must pull them into the fold.

I challenge that perspective. I don't believe our children are outside the fold when they are raised in Christian homes. They are *in* the fold.

I believe our children are born under a covenant faith relationship with God and, as such, have entrance into the throne room of God.

One day I was worshiping God, and I came to a new realization. As a child, growing up in a Christian family, the spiritual choice I had to make was this . . .

*I had to choose the God who
had already been chosen for me.*

The faith of my parents gave me access as a child to the very throne room of God. I was "at home" in His presence because of their faith relationship with Him. I didn't need to do anything other than be the son of Syvelle and Lovie

Phillips in order to pray, praise, or worship God. I had full authority as a child to pray and be heard in heaven. I had full authority to sing praise songs to Jesus. I had full authority to worship God as my Creator and Savior and Lord.

It is crucial for us to recognize that God sees our children *through* us. In like manner, God sees us through our relationship with His Son, the Lord Jesus Christ. We are viewed through the bloodline of Jesus—His shed blood on the cross. God views us as righteous because of our relationship with the righteousness of Jesus Christ. What Jesus has done for us spares us from God's wrath and puts us into a position to receive God's blessings.

Carried one step further, what we have done in accepting Jesus Christ and establishing Him as Lord of our homes puts our children under a covering of righteousness so that they are viewed as part of the family of God from their conception.

Your faith has earned your children entrance into the presence of God. You've believed for your children's relationship with the Lord. As in all things you believe for with your faith, it becomes yours as you confess it and live by it. Claim your children's privileged position in the throne room of God as a reality! See them walking and talking there in the very presence of the Almighty!

I challenge you today . . .

> *See your children as already being*
> *members of those who are covered*
> *by a covenant relationship with God.*

Isaiah 44:3–5 gives us a wonderful prophecy—the words of the Lord to Jacob His servant, and to Israel whom the Lord has chosen:

> "For I will pour water on him who is thirsty,
> And floods on the dry ground;

8

I will pour My Spirit on your descendants,
And My blessing on your offspring;
They will spring up among the grass
Like willows by the watercourses."
One will say, "I am the LORD's";
Another will call himself by the name of Jacob;
Another will write with his hand, "The LORD's,"
And name himself by the name of Israel.

What a wonderful promise of the Lord: "I will pour My Spirit on your descendants, and My blessing on your offspring."

Notice that the Lord did not say, "If your children make an early confession of faith in Me, I will do this." Neither did He say, "If your children never sin and always obey Me, I will bless them."

No, the Lord said, "I *will* pour My Spirit on your descendants, and My blessing on your offspring."

Claim that promise of the Lord for your life today. Declare, "I am the Lord's. I belong to God. The Lord is going to pour out His Spirit on my children. The Lord is going to bless my children abundantly, and they are going to spring up in Him and bear fruit for Him."

Whose Children?

Have you ever played the game with your young children in which you ask, "Whose children are you?"

The children usually respond, "Yours!"

As you teach them that little game, go one step further. Ask, "And to whom do we belong?"

"The Lord!"

The greatest proclamation each child can learn to make is, "I am the Lord's. I belong to Jesus. I am God's property."

Let your children anticipate the day when the Spirit of

9

the Lord is poured out on them. Great blessings are ahead for them!

As a parent, you can say boldly to your children, "The Spirit of God is going to be poured out on you. God has great blessings ahead for you! Now, that might not be true for you if you were born down the street into a family that doesn't love and serve the Lord. But you were born into this family. We are the Lord's people. We seek to love and serve Him. And therefore, His promise to us is that He is going to pour out His Spirit on you and bless you!"

Say that to children and watch their eyes widen and a look of hope and anticipation spread across their faces!

Principle 2:
God Desires to Bless Your Children with His Presence and Power . . . Beginning NOW

A great many researchers and commentators tell us that the rapid rise of suicides and suicide attempts among children and teens stems from an underlying feeling: a deep-seated dread about their future.

Our young people, as a whole, don't seem to have a hope that their future is going to be better than the lives of their parents. They don't have a sense that there's something good awaiting them in adulthood.

Children being raised in Christian homes should not hold to that conclusion. God has greater things for our children than they can ask or imagine. (See Eph. 3:20–21 for confirmation of that profound truth.) We need to hold out a bright future in the Lord for our children. We need to build their expectation for a future filled with God's blessing and His presence. We need to excite them about the possibilities that await them—a fulfilling and challenging role that God has designed just for them, a position in His kingdom that is just right for their particular talents, personalities, and abilities. We need to let our children know that they are irreplaceable to us and to God—that no one else can ever do the work, say the words, or fulfill the call that God has prepared just for them. Furthermore, this call of God isn't going to be too hard for them, too boring, or too draining. It will be the most exciting, most joyous, and most fulfilling thing they have ever done or could ever do.

We need to instill in them an eager anticipation for the anointing of the Holy Spirit to pour over their lives. We need to build enthusiasm in them for the blessings that God has in store *just for them!*

We need to let our children know when good things happen to us that God has the same good things in store for them today and tomorrow. God doesn't have a limited supply of blessings, rewards, or miracles. His riches in heaven are unlimited, and every good thing that He has given to you as a parent, He has in store for your children, too.

Can your children feel the anointing power of God *as children?*

Yes!

Can your children experience God's presence in their lives *as children?*

Yes!

My four-year-old daughter, Taylor, has a *very* loud voice. She does everything with gusto and with volume. We often say that she talks at eighty decibels and sings at ninety. When Taylor sings, "Our God is an awesome God," everyone within a radius of a hundred yards is affected.

Does God turn a deaf ear to her song because she is only four years old? No. I believe the Lord not only receives that praise offering but imparts a sense of His presence to Taylor every time she sings to Him.

You may say, "Phil, do you really expect children to give words of prophecy, words of wisdom, or words of knowledge? Can children manifest a gift of healing, faith, or miracles?"

I answer you with a resounding "Yes!"

These gifts of the Holy Spirit *aren't* limited to adults! Nothing in the Scriptures puts an age limit on the out-pouring of the presence of God or the gifts of the Holy Spirit.

Furthermore, there isn't a "child" version or "junior portion" of the Holy Spirit given to children. The Holy Spirit deals with children in the same way He deals with us. He convicts them. He uses them. He leads them.

Even though your children may be young, immature, and inexperienced physically, mentally, and socially, the Holy Spirit working in your children is *not* young, immature, or inexperienced.

Joel 2:28–29 confirms that to us:

And it shall come to pass afterward
That I will pour out My Spirit on all flesh;
Your sons and your daughters shall prophesy,
Your old men shall dream dreams,
Your young men shall see visions.
And also on My menservants and on My maidservants
I will pour out My Spirit in those days.

Notice the prominent role that sons and daughters play in this passage.

Let your children anticipate with joy the day when the Lord gives them prophecies, dreams, and visions. Let them look with eagerness to the time when the Holy Spirit pours out His gifts on them and manifests His fruit in their lives.

I, for one, *want* my children to prophesy, to proclaim the Lord, to be so sensitive to the Holy Spirit that they will move and speak at His prompting.

Principle 3:
God Has a Destiny for Your
Children That Began in the Womb

Hear the words of the angel to Zacharias, the father of John the Baptist, the forerunner of Jesus.

> The angel said to him, "Do not be afraid, Zacharias, for your prayer is heard; and your wife Elizabeth will bear you a son, and you shall call his name John. And you will have joy and gladness, and many will rejoice at his birth. For he will be great in the sight of the Lord, and shall drink neither wine nor strong drink. He will also be filled with the Holy Spirit, even from his mother's womb. And he will turn many of the children of Israel to the Lord their God. He will also go before Him in the spirit and power of Elijah, 'to turn the hearts of the fathers to the children,' and the disobedient to the wisdom of the just, to make ready a people prepared for the Lord" (Luke 1:13–17).

Note two important things about this passage.

First, Zacharias and Elizabeth did not have the benefit of knowing the Messiah, accepting the sacrifice of Jesus on the cross, or receiving the outpouring of the Holy Spirit in their lives. Yet, Elizabeth's womb was the workplace of the Holy Spirit. How much more so are the wombs of our Christian women a place where the Holy Spirit begins His work in our lives. If John the Baptist was filled with the Holy Spirit from his mother's womb, what are we believing for our children?

We are learning more and more about the importance of prenatal care, not only physical care but emotional and spiritual care. Mothers transmit more than nutrients to their young. A "spirit"—an emotional strength—can be transferred to a child still in the womb. This spiritual impartation becomes the very foundation of the child's psyche. It is the basis on which the personality is formed.

The Jews knew that. Pregnant women often went on spiritual retreats during the first few months of their pregnancy, primarily to pray for and sing to the child in the womb. The song of Mary, which we read in Luke 1:46–55, may well be such a prenatal prayer that Mary prayed for the beloved Son being formed in her womb. It is a prophetic word about the nature of Jesus, even before His birth.

As soon as you discover that you are to be the parent of a child, begin to pray for that child. Speak to that child in the name of the Lord. Prophesy over your child—proclaiming the good things of God and the perfection of the Lord's will in your child's life. Sing praise and worship choruses to the baby in the womb. Establish even before your child's birth a consistent pattern of spiritual nourishment. Recognize that the Holy Spirit is at work in the life of your child, even while your child is still in the womb.

"But," you may say, "my child isn't called to be John the Baptist."

In many ways, your child *is* called to be a forerunner of the Lord—to prepare the way so that others may come to the Lord, to be great in the sight of the Lord. When we see our children as potential servants of God, chosen and created with a special place in the kingdom of God already ordained for them, we, too, will have greater "joy and gladness" at the birth of our children. We'll be in eager anticipation from the day of their birth to see how the Lord will manifest Himself in them and through them.

Second, the purpose of John the Baptist was to turn the children of Israel back to God, and to turn the hearts of the fathers to the children. This passage of Scripture is in direct relationship to Malachi 4:5–6, the final words of the Old Testament, which says that the one who comes just before the day of the Lord's appearing will have as his mission to "turn the hearts of the fathers to the children, and the hearts of the children to their fathers."

Your children's purpose on the earth today is also one of turning hearts. As we believers today anticipate the Lord's return, we find ourselves in the same position as those who were alive preceding the Lord's first appearing. Our role is to turn hearts toward the Lord and toward one another. Ours is a healing mission—to bring people back into right relationship with one another and, ultimately, into right relationship with the Father.

Children can, and are destined to, do this work.

Principle 4:
God Intends for Your Children to
Learn and Walk in His Principles . . . NOW

We are called to bring our children into a deep walk with God, not a walk that is simplistic or superficial. Too often, we sell our children's ability to absorb spiritual principles far too short!

The Bible has dozens of passages in which we find the words *little children* or *little ones.* As I've traveled this nation and talked to both pastors and laypersons alike, I've asked repeatedly, "Do you think this passage should be taken literally or allegorically? Do you think this passage refers to children or to those who are young in their faith?" Nearly everyone has said, "Oh, those passages mean the young in faith." In so concluding, they seem to discount the applicability of the passage to real live children.

I disagree heartily. I believe that virtually every one of the biblical passages in which we are admonished to behave in a certain way toward little ones can refer equally to flesh-and-blood children. We should read these passages as referring to *both* the spiritually young and the physically young.

The fact is, the physically young who are being raised in the church, and who are ideally being raised in families by parents who call themselves Christian, are also spiritually young.

They are growing up in Christ.

They are His "little children."

They are the "little ones."

Let's not dismiss them from our understanding of how to apply the Scriptures but include them as the *majority* of those addressed within the church as being young in the faith.

Begin to see your children today growing in understanding and grace. See them already in a transformation process to become ever more like Christ Jesus.

Our desire as parents must be that we want our children to love and serve the Lord every day of their lives. Not just every day of their teenage lives or their adult lives. But *every* day of their lives, beginning now.

When you truly gain insight into your children's position with Jesus, your behavior toward them will change. You will no longer look for them to grow up so they can accept Jesus. You will see them as already accepted by Him, and you will look for them to grow up *in* Him.

Ask yourself today . . .

Have I dedicated my children to the Lord but am awaiting that day when they accept the Lord before I consider them to be full members of the body of Christ?

Or . . .

Am I expecting my children to grow every day more and more into the likeness of Jesus Christ as full members of His body?

Your Perspective Does Make a Difference

You may say, "Phil, does it really matter if I perceive my children as persons waiting to be born again or think of them as persons who are already in full communion with God?"

It makes all the difference in the world!

The parent who perceives the children as being "on spiritual hold"—waiting to be born again at a future date when they are "accountable" or "adult"—tends to think these things:

1. My role as a parent is to provide information about God rather than to invite my children to share my relationship with God.

2. As a Christian parent, I have more of God than my children have. My children are still on the outside of an intense love relationship with the Lord. I'm on the inside. It's my job, therefore, to pull my children in out of the cold so they can experience what I have.

3. As a Christian parent, I must do everything I can to put my children into a position where they can accept Jesus at the earliest possible age, and thereby, I can see them saved.

Parents with this mind-set tend to act on their beliefs in these ways:

• They insist that their children read the Bible and go to Sunday school and study God's Word because doing these things is "good for them"—not because they are the most exciting things anyone can do.

• They continually call to recognition their children's sins in hopes of building an awareness of sin that will lead to repentance of sin. Think about it for a moment. How many times have you heard a parent say, "That's really wrong; God wouldn't like that"? The picture painted of God is one of a very stern God who tends to say no more than Mom and Dad do.

• They drag or push their children to every possible event that they believe might bring about a conversion—be it youth rallies, church camp, vacation Bible school, or even participation in altar calls—all with a hope that something will "hook" their children and bring them to a salvation experience.

The net result is one giant load of guilt and conviction. And ninety-nine times out of a hundred, the outcome of guilt is to push persons away rather than to pull them toward the desired result!

Let's consider now the parent who perceives the children as already being under a covenant relationship and, therefore, in full standing and in full communion before God. Such a parent tends to think:

1. My role as a parent is to share fully my relationship with the Lord with my children.

2. As a parent, I am to make certain that each member of our family experiences as much of God as possible, every day, many times a day.

3. As a parent, I am to foster the spiritual development of my children so that they might grow daily from grace to grace and learn more about who Jesus is, how God works, what God expects of His chosen people and, above all, how much God loves them.

Parents who hold to these beliefs tend to display these behaviors:

• They include their children in all spiritual activities in which they themselves participate. When the parents praise, the children praise. When the parents intercede in prayer, the children intercede. When the parents engage in acts of Christian service, the children are invited along.

• They foster a daily walk-and-talk experience with Jesus. The name of Jesus is brought up frequently. Prayer is spontaneous in seeking God's direction or help. Words of praise and thanksgiving are frequently on the lips of all family members. In all, there's an expectation that the children will comprehend and experience a spiritual reality of God's presence.

I have met a number of young children who have said to

me, in essence, "Jesus lives with us." They truly believe Jesus is a member of the family because so much of the family conversation is about Him or is directed to Him. Young children do not separate the real physical world from the real spiritual world as we adults tend to do. Something can be just as real in their imaginations as it is in the concrete material realm. What a wonderful attribute that is, and one we should avoid trampling upon. Children's awareness of the spiritual realm is keen. They can know and experience the reality of God's power and presence in a way that is very real to them. Wise Christian parents encourage that walk-and-talk relationship with Jesus Christ.

• They bring their children with them to church events because of what those events might contribute to spiritual growth. The parental question after such an event is not "Did you get saved?" but "What did the Lord teach you?" The children are regarded as spiritual beings capable of giving back to the body of Christ their unique and valuable insights. The children are included in all aspects of the rituals, and their attendance is valued.

What is the net result here? Rather than guilt and conviction, the children feel acceptance, love, warmth, and involvement in a community of faith—the community of faith in their own family as well as a community of faith outside their immediate family unit. They feel plugged in, not shut out. They feel themselves to be legitimate members of the body of Christ, not sinners awaiting entrance. They feel invited to stretch and grow spiritually rather than nervous about making a mistake before God.

Moreover . . .

The children who grow up feeling an integral part of the spiritual life of their family and church are children who will never want to be separated from that depth of love and acceptance!

The children will not have to be pulled, kicking and screaming, to an altar of repentance. They will already be at the altar, ready to respond quickly and obediently to the gentle call of the Holy Spirit in their lives.

In sum . . .

Children can tell how you believe about them. They can feel if you consider them equal members of the body of Christ. They know if you consider them second-class spiritual citizens. They sense your rejection, your distance, at a very deep emotional level.

Conversely, children can tell if you include them as full participants in your spiritual life, withholding nothing from them that comes from the Lord.

Who Is
Really Out?

If we see our children outside the fold, we must also automatically see them in dire danger of being snared by the enemy of our souls, who also lives apart from the grace and mercy of God. Such children, then, are the devil's prey.

Many parents hold to precisely that position. They believe the devil and his cohorts are ready to pounce on their children at every turn. They live in fear that their children might be taken away in death or be otherwise destroyed here on the earth.

If we begin to see our children inside the fold, however, our perspective changes dramatically. We then view our children safe and secure in the arms of Jesus. The enemy is someone against whom our entire family must unite to defeat. We engage in a struggle of us against him instead of parent against an ungodly alliance of devil and children.

The difference in perspective plays out in subtle ways.

George and Ann for many years regarded their son as unprotected prey of the enemy. Ann lived in nearly constant fear that the devil would destroy her child before he reached the age of accountability. She said to me, "I felt fine when my son was an infant, but as soon as he began to exert his own will, I felt as if he was unprotected spiritually, almost as if he was wandering on his own in a dangerous forest."

George and Ann warned their son, Cal, continually about evil but gave him pitifully few skills with which to defeat his, and their, spiritual enemy. The result? Cal picked up on the fear of his parents and in turn became fearful of all things spiritual—including fear of a powerful and demanding God. To counteract this fear, he began to rely on his own power, and as he reached his teen years, he began to "dare" the devil. Even after Cal accepted Jesus as his Savior during a revival service, he continued to live in a weakened position spiritually, as if he was always looking over his shoulder for the enemy's next strike. Years after a sound conversion experience, he continued to question whether he was truly saved in a way that was definitive and lasting.

Linda and William, on the other hand, viewed their son on their side spiritually from the moment of his conception. He was regarded as a fellow warrior of the faith even when he was just a toddler. From this perspective, Linda and Will taught their child how to pray with faith, how to resist the devil, and how to build up his faith by reading God's Word and establishing a daily prayer relationship with the Lord.

The day came, at about age eight, when their son, Peter, felt a need to openly confess Jesus as his own personal Savior and Lord. He did so as the next step in his faith walk.

Peter didn't begin to learn to pray at that point. He already knew how to pray. He didn't begin to believe God would protect him and deliver him. He already had dozens of experiences in his past that he could point to and say with assurance, "I know God was with me then."

Peter grew in his faith from "strength to strength," just as the Bible challenges us to grow.

Can you see the difference?

Children who are made to feel separate from their parents' faith inevitably feel less secure and are invariably less comfortable in the Lord's presence. Children who are made to feel a part of a spiritual family team feel deeply secure and are "at home" with the heavenly Father.

The reality is also that the devil is more soundly defeated in a family that sees itself as a spiritual unit. The faith of children combined with the faith of parents—in coming against evil and standing strong for righteousness—is a powerful faith. Spiritual family unity brings great family victory. I've seen it happen over and over again. When the children are included in spiritual warfare—parents and children uniting in spirit against the enemy coming against their family—the family wins, the devil flees, and faith is built up in both parents and children.

In a nutshell—put the devil out of your spiritual family and keep your children in it.

Must Children Go Through a Rebellious Stage?

I meet many parents who seem to believe that their children are in some way protected spiritually until they begin to think for themselves and rebel against God, at which point they begin a period of wandering aimlessly and dangerously in sin until they fall on their knees at an altar and weep tears of repentance. It's as if they expect their children to rebel spiritually as a normal part of growing up.

That is not my perspective. I believe our children can and should walk in faith expecting and accepting more of God's presence into their lives month after month, year after year, until their faith has developed fully and they openly, with full spiritual knowledge, confess Jesus Christ as their own personal Savior and Lord.

I do *not* believe that children need to rebel or to live in rebellion for a single day. I do *not* believe that children need to fall away from the faith of their parents before they can come to an awareness of a need for salvation, an act of repentance, or an experience of being born spiritually.

Are there biblical precedents for my view? I believe that most of the Bible points toward the reality of household salvation.

Perhaps the most famous example is that of the parable of the prodigal son told by our Lord Jesus. Let me share this parable with you in its entirety:

A certain man had two sons. And the younger of them said to his father, "Father, give me the portion of goods that falls to me." So he divided to them his livelihood. And not many days after, the younger son gathered all together, journeyed to a far country, and there wasted his possessions with prodigal living.

But when he had spent all, there arose a severe famine in that land, and he began to be in want. Then he went and joined himself to a citizen of that country, and he sent him into his fields to feed swine. And he would gladly have filled his stomach with the pods that the swine ate, and no one gave him anything.

But when he came to himself, he said, "How many of my father's hired servants have bread enough and to spare, and I perish with hunger! I will arise and go to my father, and will say to him, 'Father, I have sinned against heaven and before you, and I am no longer worthy to be called your son. Make me like one of your hired servants.' "

And he arose and came to his father. But when he was still a great way off, his father saw him and had compassion, and ran and fell on his neck and kissed him. And the son said to him, "Father, I have sinned against heaven and in

23

your sight, and am no longer worthy to be called your son." But the father said to his servants, "Bring out the best robe and put it on him, and put a ring on his hand and sandals on his feet. And bring the fatted calf here and kill it, and let us eat and be merry; for this my son was dead and is alive again; he was lost and is found." And they began to be merry.

Now his older son was in the field. And as he came and drew near to the house, he heard music and dancing. So he called one of the servants and asked what these things meant. And he said to him, "Your brother has come, and because he has received him safe and sound, your father has killed the fatted calf."

But he was angry and would not go in. Therefore his father came out and pleaded with him. So he answered and said to his father, "Lo, these many years I have been serving you; I never transgressed your commandment at any time; and yet you never gave me a young goat, that I might make merry with my friends. But as soon as this son of yours came, who has devoured your livelihood with harlots, you killed the fatted calf for him."

And he said to him, "Son, you are always with me, and all that I have is yours. It was right that we should make merry and be glad, for your brother was dead and is alive again, and was lost and is found" (Luke 15:11–32).

On the surface, this parable may seem to support the view that our children must rebel and leave home before they come to a full knowledge of and acceptance of the Lord Jesus. But look again, this time at the older brother who did *not* rebel. Here is God's true plan. The father says, "Son, you are always with me, and all that I have is yours." That is the position God desires to have with each of His children—that we might *never* rebel, *never* leave, *never* forsake Him. His will is that we might always be with Him

24

and have access to all that is His! The Lord makes a provision for the redemption of the prodigal. His heart's desire and His highest will, however, are that none of His little ones becomes a prodigal.

Making a Commitment to a New Vision of Your Children

Ask God today to build up your faith for your children and to help you see them with His eyes.

Ask Him very specifically to

• give you a vision of your children in Him.

• give you a vision of your children serving the Lord all the days of their lives.

• give you a vision of your children praising and worshiping the Lord with a fullness of spirit.

• give you a vision of your children loving others and bringing them to a knowledge of the Lord.

• give you a vision of your children having children and passing on to *them* the faith walk that has been established in their own lives.

Ask the Lord to confirm to you that your seed will not be diminished or fall into sin but that your heirs *will* follow after righteousness.

And then, take a second important step. Believe that the Lord will do what He has planted within you as a vision. Trust Him to fulfill His Word in your life, that He will be faithful to the end toward which He has called you and your family, and that He will perform all of His promises to you.

3

Seeing Your Household
as Belonging to the Lord

Gather the people together, men and women and little ones, and the stranger who is within your gates, that they may hear and that they may learn to fear the LORD your God and carefully observe all the words of this law, and that their children, who have not known it, may hear and learn to fear the LORD your God as long as you live in the land which you cross the Jordan to possess.
—Deuteronomy 31:12–13

God's primary method for establishing His people on the earth is through our families and raising up godly children.

I believe this method supersedes all other evangelistic and mission outreaches. Now, please understand that I am in no way putting down these efforts. I grew up in a family that was intensely involved in missions and evangelism. I am an evangelist. Missions and evangelism, however, aren't God's *primary* plan. His primary method through the ages has been the establishment of one generation after another of believers. The foremost and most obvious way that happens, and should happen, is through families and the training up of godly children to be godly adults, who will in turn bear and train godly children to be godly adults, and so on.

This principle is stated in Acts 2:39: "For the promise is to you and to your children, and to all who are afar off, as many as the Lord our God will call." The promise is *first* to you and your children and then to those who are afar off.

In fact, I will go so far as to say that the foremost purpose of marriage is that men and women might train up godly children, either through bearing natural children or birthing spiritual children. The Lord made this statement about marriage:

> She is your companion
> And your wife by covenant.
> But did He not make them one,
> Having a remnant of the Spirit?
> And why one?
> He seeks godly offspring.
> Therefore take heed to your spirit,
> And let none deal treacherously with the wife
>   of his youth (Mal. 2:14–15).

That word *remnant* is translated in the King James Version as "residue." Residue is something that is left on, stuck on, left behind. The Holy Spirit within us has that quality. He's stuck to us. He's a part of us, and as such, He becomes a part of our marriages, a part of our families, and a part of our children's lives from before their conception.

Godly offspring! What a noble goal has been set before us as Christian parents today.

Before that will happen, however, we must see our families—our households—as God sees them.

I'd like to share with you seven key principles related to our families, as drawn from the Word of God.

Family Principle 1:
God Established the Family as
a Vehicle Leading to Redemption

Genesis 1:27–28 declares,

> So God created man in His own image; in the image of
> God He created him; male and female He created them.
> Then God blessed them, and God said to them, "Be fruitful
> and multiply; fill the earth and subdue it; have dominion
> over the fish of the sea, over the birds of the air, and over
> every living thing that moves on the earth."

God designed human beings to reflect His image. Unless
we have a real faith in God, that could almost sound like
blasphemy when we look at the degenerative state of humanity today. Nevertheless, God designed human beings
to reflect who He is.

God gave human beings dominion, a mind, a spirit. He
said, "Let Us make man in Our image" (Gen. 1:26). He
created people in consultation with Jesus and the Holy
Spirit—as if reflecting upon and pondering this decision.
Everything else, God simply spoke into existence. For humankind, God molded the earth and breathed into the
form His own breath. His relationship with humankind
from the very beginning was one that was anticipated with
warm fellowship and intimacy. His relationship with humankind was always rooted and grounded in love.

From the very beginning, God intended for us to be His
sons and daughters. The family was God's idea from the
outset. "Let Us" speaks of a family relationship. Human
beings were to be added to the divine family. Every provision was made for us to have that unique and privileged
role among all other created beings.

Of all the things that fell with the sin of Adam and Eve
—the perfection of the Garden, the eternal nature of their

bodies, the face-to-face fellowship with God—the concept of family did not fall. In fact, through a family relationship and the birth of a child, God provided a means for the broken relationship He had experienced with humankind to be restored!

The family today is the most powerfully protecting force against sin and the strongest motivating force for righteousness we have. It was God's design for the family to be the primary tool for establishing His presence and His power on this earth. God intends for righteous men and women to be born and raised within godly families.

I hope you will let this revelation of God's Word sink deep into your spirit. The primary force for the redemption of humanity, and the furtherance of God's kingdom on the earth today, is *not* the church, *not* a foreign missions program, *not* an evangelistic ministry. It is the family.

In fact, the church and all of its various ministries were established to help families do their job. Church leaders—prophets, apostles, evangelists, pastors, teachers—are God's support system for families.

The *first* thing that God did in response to human need was to create the family (Gen. 2:20–24). When God saw Adam without "a helper comparable to him," God did not create the church: He created the family. The church exists primarily to help the family love, honor, and serve God!

You may say, "Well, what about people who don't grow up in godly families?" God's provision was that those who came to know Him in a way other than through their own families might be *adopted* into a larger family of God. Not only do we become the adopted sons and daughters of our heavenly Father when we repent of our sins and accept Jesus as our eternal sacrifice, our Lord, and our older brother before God . . . but we become sons and daughters of the faith. We are to be members incorporate of Christ's body—brothers and sisters in the spirit, with spiritual mothers and fathers who will nurture us and train us. The primary analogy of the church is that of a family!

The Lord Jesus Himself said this about those who gave up their ungodly family lives to follow Him:

> Assuredly, I say to you, there is no one who has left house or brothers or sisters or father or mother or wife or children or lands, for My sake and the gospel's, who shall not receive a hundredfold now in this time—houses and brothers and sisters and mothers and children and lands, with persecutions—and in the age to come, eternal life (Mark 10:29–30).

Therefore, when we emphasize the family, we are in line with what God intended from the creation of the world.

Family Principle 2:
The Decisions of a Parent Determine the Spiritual Direction and Fate of the Family

We learn from Genesis 5:

> This is the book of the genealogy of Adam. In the day that God created man, He made him in the likeness of God. He created them male and female, and blessed them and called them Mankind in the day they were created. And Adam lived one hundred and thirty years, and begot a son in his own likeness (vv. 1–3).

What was God's likeness? It was pure holiness and righteousness. That was the image of Adam before he sinned. After Adam sinned, however, and was cast away from the Garden and the perfection and abiding presence of God, Adam no longer reflected God's image of holiness and righteousness. His very nature had changed to that of sin. The firstborn son of Adam was not a model of righteousness and holiness. On the contrary! He became a murderer and a fugitive!

It was only upon the birth of Enosh, Adam's grandson, that people again turned to God and began to rely upon Him. The Scriptures say, "Then men began to call upon the name of the LORD" (Gen. 4:26).

Believe me, the birth of a child calls you to reevaluate your faith and your standing with God as nothing else does!

There you are, thinking that you are a mighty man or woman of God, and along comes a few pounds of willful flesh, born in your likeness with your initial sin nature of "I, me, and mine." Suddenly, you are confronted with the fact that you may be little more than a spiritual wimp. For the next twenty years, you face the challenge of passing your faith to the next generation—the challenge of creating a home and a family relationship that will become a pathway toward heaven for your child.

The babies to whom you have given your genes will require your entire life. They will demand your time and attention, not for a few seconds but continually. They will study your every move. And they will follow in the footsteps of the life you model for them, basing most of their behavior *not* on what you say but on what you do. Your children will literally become your students, learning from what you do and are.

Indeed, that gives pause for soul-searching reflection.

Family Principle 3: God Sees the Family as a Unit of One

One of my earliest memories is of my father saying, "God doesn't call a man into the ministry. He calls a family." How so? Because all family members are in a position to experience all of the results of a ministry role—both good and bad.

Perhaps no biblical example more clearly illustrates this principle than the life of Noah: "Then the Lord said to Noah, 'Come into the ark, you and all your household, because I have seen that you are righteous before Me in this generation'" (Gen. 7:1). And the writer of Hebrews reinforces the thought: "By faith Noah, being divinely warned of things not yet seen, moved with godly fear, prepared an ark for the saving of his household, by which he condemned the world and became heir of the righteousness which is according to faith" (11:7).

The ark is a spiritual "type" for our homes today. In reality, Noah's ark was a dwelling place of refuge constructed in the midst of a society in which God had found only wickedness, a society in which the thoughts of the human heart were only evil continually, a society about which God expressed grief and sorrow at humanity's creation.

The ark was a means of God's grace, of His unmerited favor in a time of judgment. It is the first instance in Scripture where we see God providing a means of absolute escape from evil that includes an entire family and is based on the righteousness of a parent. Noah's family—his wife and all three sons and their wives—are saved from destruction as the floodwaters sweep over the earth. They are given God's command to replenish the earth and to be fruitful and multiply. Again God says to them that "in the image of God He made man," and He commands them to "bring forth abundantly in the earth" (Gen. 9:6, 7). It is with this family—tne Scriptures say that God spoke to Noah *and* to his sons—that God makes a covenant never again to destroy the earth with a flood.

Let's consider for a moment, however, what happens after the Flood. Ham, the middle son, sins. He becomes the father of Canaan and, as such, reestablishes idolatry on the earth.

Why did God allow Ham to be rescued from the floodwaters if he was only going to reintroduce blatant sin into the world? Surely Ham's sinful nature didn't just blossom overnight once the ark had safely landed on dry ground. Couldn't God have foreseen Ham's behavior?

The answer is simply that God spared Ham because of Noah's righteousness. Ham, by himself, deserved to be destroyed with the rest of humankind. Ham, as Noah's son, was in a position to be saved. The Scriptures declare, "Then the Lord said to *Noah,* 'Come into the ark, *you* and all *your* household, because I have seen that *you* are righteous before Me in this generation" (Gen. 7:1, emphasis added).

Noah covered Ham with his faith, even though later Ham, in his sin, would uncover Noah.

In sparing Noah and his entire family and in making a covenant with them, God established a pattern that will continue throughout the remaining chapters of Genesis and the subsequent sixty-five books of the Bible. God sees the family as a unit of ONE.

Family Principle 4:
God Intends Faith to Be Passed Down as a Family Inheritance

Later in Genesis we read,

> After these things the word of the Lord came to Abram in a vision, saying, "Do not be afraid, Abram. I am your shield, your exceedingly great reward." But Abram said, "Lord God, what will You give me, seeing I go childless, and the heir of my house is Eliezer of Damascus?" Then Abram said, "Look, You have given me no offspring; indeed one born in my house is my heir!" And behold, the word of the Lord came to him, saying, "This one shall not be your heir,

but one who will come from your own body shall be your heir" (Gen. 15:1–4).

Prior to that encounter, God told Abram on three separate occasions that he would have a son. Abram had been in a faith-building process, which as we all know is not always a comfortable process. He was nearing ninety years of age, and God continued to say, "You will have a son." He went on to say, "Look now toward heaven, and count the stars if you are able to number them." And He said to Abram, "So shall your descendants be" (Gen. 15:5).

Notice God's plan:

• First, God *desired* for Abram to have a "faith" family. The heir, so to speak, in Abram's home was an heir of human design—a servant, not a son. It is always God's desire for us to bear children in *faith*, whether they are natural children or spiritual children.

• Second, God intended for Abram's son to have children. He intended for one generation of faith to spawn another generation of faith.

What does this plan mean to you and me as parents today? It means that God is on our side! He longs for your children to grow up in His care and keeping just as much as you long for that. He desires for your children to call Him, "Abba, Father"—or "Daddy God"—just as much as you long to hear your children affectionately call you "Daddy" or "Mommy."

Furthermore, God intends and desires for your children so to grow up in Him that they will desire to have faith children of their own, continuing the progeny of God from one generation to many generations, until the people of God are too numerous to count. What a wonderful future God envisions for you as a parent and for your children as parents someday!

When we look at Abram, we see that God had spent

twenty-five years building up faith in him for his son, Isaac.

Do you have faith for your children today?

Our Covenant Relationship with the Lord Is Rooted in the Family

Not only did God spend twenty-five years building up the faith of Abraham, but He established a covenant with Abraham that from the very outset included Abraham's unborn son.

The covenant was God's method of establishing a relationship with His people. God first established a relationship with an individual, then with that individual's immediate family, and finally with that individual's descendants. The covenant with Abraham, for example, was entered into with Abraham as an individual (Gen. 12:1–2) and then extended to Abraham and his family (Gen. 15:9–18) and was renewed with Abraham's grandson, Jacob (Gen. 28:13–15), and ultimately with one of Abraham's descendants, Moses (Exod. 3:6; 24:3–8).

We Christians very often say that Christianity is not so much a religion as a relationship. We tend to think of that relationship as being only with individuals. Throughout the Scriptures, the relationship is usually couched in terms of family.

God's unfolding revelation to Abraham was one intended for Isaac's blessing, and then for Isaac to be a blessing to others . . . just as Abraham was blessed to be a blessing. (See Gen. 12:3.)

What a comfort it is to recognize that God's plan is for your children today to have been birthed not only into your natural family but also into your faith relationship with the heavenly Father. Your children are born into the covenant relationship you have with God. They grow up not outside that covenant relationship but inside it. And finally, what a joy to anticipate that God looks ahead to the day when your grandchildren and great-grandchildren and great-great-grandchildren will be serving Him.

In brief summary, then, the Scriptures present an ongoing revelation, from generation to generation, of God's plan for families on this earth.

• In the story of Adam and Eve, we see that God has set the family upon the earth as an integral part of His method for fellowship with men and women. Our families are the crucible for redemption and for developing faith. Our homes can be a gateway to righteousness for our children. If we fail to follow God's directives in our lives, however, our homes can become a gateway to sin. Nothing bears as much influence on the future spiritual health of your children as does the spiritual atmosphere of your home.

• In the story of Noah, we see that God blesses an entire family through the righteousness of a godly parent. God's grace is extended to all family members because of parental righteousness, even to a family member with an idolatrous heart.

• In the story of Abraham, we see that God spent twenty-five years building up Abraham's faith for his offspring. God intends not only for Abraham to bear a faith son, Isaac, but for Isaac in turn to bear faith children who will ultimately be as numerous as the stars of the sky. The relationship between Abraham and God is one of covenant. Isaac is born into that covenant, not apart from it. Indeed, he is an heir of the covenant.

Family Principle 5:
God Has Provided for the
Salvation of Households

The apostle Peter tells us that Jesus Christ is our Passover Lamb: "You were not redeemed with corruptible things, like silver or gold, from your aimless conduct received by tradition from your fathers, but with the precious blood of Christ, as of a lamb without blemish and without spot" (1 Pet. 1:18–19).

The clearest picture we have in the Bible of who Jesus is for us—our Redeemer and Savior—is the picture of Him as our Passover Lamb.

Let's refresh our memory of that story in Exodus:

Now the LORD spoke to Moses and Aaron in the land of Egypt, saying, "This month shall be your beginning of months; it shall be the first month of the year to you. Speak to the congregation of Israel, saying: 'On the tenth day of this month every man shall take for himself a lamb, according to the house of his father, a lamb for a household. And if the household is too small for the lamb, let him and his neighbor next to his house take it according to the number of the persons; according to each man's need you shall make your count for the lamb. Your lamb shall be without blemish, a male. . . . And they shall take some of the blood and put it on the two doorposts and on the lintel of the houses where they eat it. . . .

And thus you shall eat it: with a belt on your waist, your sandals on your feet, and your staff in your hand. So you shall eat it in haste. It is the LORD's Passover. For I will pass through the land of Egypt on that night, and will strike all the firstborn in the land of Egypt, both man and beast; and against all the gods of Egypt I will execute judgment: I am the LORD. Now the blood shall be a sign for you on the houses where you are. And when I see the blood, I will pass over you; and the plague shall not be on you to destroy you when I strike the land of Egypt' " (Exod. 12:1–7, 11–13).

I'd like to call your attention to four things about this Passover scene.

First, the analogy to Jesus and the Lord's "Passover" in our lives is clear. Jesus, without sin, is our male lamb without blemish. His blood dripping from the cross is analogous to the blood being on the doorposts and lintels of the houses. Our acceptance of His shed blood as our atoning sacrifice also spares us from God's judgment, and it separates us from the evil culture around us.

Second, notice that the Passover lamb is *not* killed and consumed on an individual basis. Its blood is not applied to individuals or to individual belongings. The lamb is killed per *household* and is to be consumed per *household,* and the blood is to be applied to the entrance of the *house.*

Should one family not be large enough to consume a single lamb by itself, it is to unite with another family. The Passover is a family event.

Third, the very purpose of the sacrifice of the Passover lamb is to ensure the safety of the family's *children.* The children in danger in this scene are the firstborn children —who, throughout Scripture, are considered to be the prime inheritors of a family's name, wealth, and status in the nation. The responsibility of the firstborn, however, is to protect the other children in the family and to be responsible for their provision. Thus, if the firstborn is eliminated, all the children are put at risk.

Can you see the spiritual analogy here? Our children are the inheritors of our faith. They are the recipients of our family's identity as Christians. They inherit our spiritual wealth and our position as the preserving salt in our nation. If *our* children are destroyed, all of the children in our nation—and, ultimately, our world—lose out.

Fourth, once the Passover lamb had been killed and its blood applied to the doorpost, it was to be eaten by the entire family: "Then they shall eat the flesh on that night; roasted in fire, with unleavened bread and with bitter herbs they shall eat it. . . . You shall let none of it remain until morning, and what remains of it until morning you shall burn with fire" (Exod. 12:8, 10).

The children are included in this feast. They are full partakers of the sacrifice that the parents have made. Unleavened bread is bread without yeast, and since yeast was considered synonymous with fermentation and sin, the unleavened bread might be considered to represent sin-free nourishment. Our children are not only to consume the sacrifice of Jesus made on behalf of our families, but they are to be raised in a sin-free atmosphere—an atmosphere that is not fermenting or seething with anger, hatred, abuse, or other ungodly behaviors.

Note, too, that the feast includes "bitter herbs." These herbs represent the sorrow involved in this event. They call attention to the fact that others outside the family of God are in dire danger, and that evil results in judgment. Our children, too, must be raised with this awareness of sin and its consequences—not that they partake of sin, but that they are made aware that sin exists, and that sin ultimately results in death, decay, and destruction. We are to nurture in our children a sense of sorrow for the world's sins and, in that, a desire to reach out to others and to rescue them from the snare and the pit before them. In sum, we are to foster a spirit of evangelism and soul winning in our children.

Furthermore, the feast was to be consumed with a spirit of readiness. The Israelites were to eat with a sense of imminent departure, a keen awareness that the Spirit of God was about to lead them from a position of bondage to a place of blessing. They were to be dressed and ready to go.

In a spiritual sense, our children must be taught from an early age that God is leading us ever onward to a place of greater and greater blessing. We must be quick in responding to Him—ever ready to obey and move out as He leads. When the nation of Israel moved out the following morning to leave Egypt forever, the children moved out, too. They were not left behind: "Then the children of Israel journeyed from Rameses to Succoth, about six hundred thousand men on foot, besides children" (Exod. 12:37).

Have you ever traveled anywhere with children on foot? No strollers. No backpacks. Simply walking with children?

Who sets the pace? It isn't the adults! Adults who walk with children walk at the children's pace. The spiritual analogy here is a precious one. We are never to outpace the spiritual children in our midst, including the spiritual children who are also natural children. Our entire forward motion as a body of Christ must be geared to the "least among us." We aren't to leave anybody behind.

Is a Bible lesson too complicated for the spiritually youngest person in the group to understand? Then the Bible lesson should be made simpler.

Is the sermon too complex for the spiritually youngest person in the group to absorb or to apply? Then the sermon should be made clearer.

Is the event too formal or too long for the spiritually youngest person to appreciate its beauty and meaning? Then the event should be scaled back or its symbolism explained.

The Israelites left Egypt, walking, with their children. Looking ahead forty years in the story, we see that the children entered the Promised Land—and had over the course of the generation developed the necessary faith for destroying God's enemies and moving into the fullness of God's blessing.

By walking spiritually at the pace of the children, you not only exalt their position and build up their spiritual esteem and confidence, but you prepare them for a future as spiritual warriors and the establishers of a faith community that is not shackled by a slave mind-set to evil.

Finally, the purpose of the Passover was to be worship. Moses said, "When your children say to you, 'What do you mean by this service?' that you shall say, 'It is the Passover sacrifice of the LORD, who passed over the houses of the children of Israel in Egypt when He struck the Egyptians and delivered our households.' " Note again that word *households*. And the passage concludes, "So the people bowed their heads and worshiped" (Exod. 12:26–27).

The Passover was a feast that separated God's people from Egypt. It was as if a giant line had been marked on the nation, with God's people on one side and the Egyptians on the other. This event, more than any other event in the Bible, delineated God's people *as* God's people. It gave them an identity, and it set them apart in their own minds and hearts as God's chosen ones.

The shed blood of Jesus does the same in our lives and in our homes. It sets us apart. It gives us our identity.

A Christian home isn't just another home. It isn't like every other home. A Christian home is distinctive. It operates according to a different set of principles. It reflects a distinctive ethic. It has a different atmosphere.

And our response to God when we recognize what He has done for us—calling us and choosing us and blessing us as His own—must be worship. We bow before Him in thanksgiving and praise, recognizing not only in our minds but in our hearts His sovereignty over our lives. His provision. His counsel. His rulership. His ownership. His protection. His eternal loving kindness as not only *the* God but *our* God.

Worship is the hallmark of the truly Christian home.

What do I mean by worship in a very practical day-to-day reality? I mean an exalting of who God is and who He desires to be in relationship with us, a recognition by all members of the family that our lives come from and are ruled by God.

Of course, that does not mean family members walk around the house every waking moment with their hands lifted, uttering words of worship to God. (It does mean that this is possible at any moment *should* any member of the family want to do this.)

On a practical level, a home characterized by worship means that all members of the family live in an attitude of worship in their hearts. They know, deep within, that God rules their household. They recognize that God has set their family apart from the wickedness of the world to be His place of refuge. They know with a deep certainty born of faith that God is on their side—He has called them for His purposes, and He will equip them to fulfill their destiny as individuals and as a family. They rely on God to meet their needs. They sense His presence among them. They obey His words to them. They are grateful for all that He has done, is doing, and will do on their behalf.

The Christian home truly must be one in which God is viewed as heavenly Father and supreme Lord. Everything is done in subjection to His will. All decisions are based on His desires. All behaviors are evaluated according to His commandments. The atmosphere is one in which spontaneous praise is welcome at any moment. The environment is one in which His peace prevails.

Is that possible? Absolutely.

Is that desirable? Above all riches. There's no more secure place to be than in a home where worship abounds—surrounded by those you love who are of like mind and heart, resting in the prevailing presence of the Almighty. There's also no more freeing atmosphere where each person is encouraged to explore full uniqueness and potential in the Lord because there's a recognition that the Lord is over all, in all, and working through all.

Remembering Our Passover

Passover, of course, is not a once-in-history event. It has been reenacted every year since its inception. The Lord set it as an annual feast so that His people might never forget it:

> And you shall tell your son in that day, saying, "This is done because of what the LORD did for me when I came up from Egypt." It shall be as a sign to you on your hand and as a memorial between your eyes, that the LORD's law may be in your mouth; for with a strong hand the LORD has brought you out of Egypt (Exod. 13:8–9).

(Even today, by the way, Jewish people keep Passover primarily as a family celebration. As a part of the ceremony, a member of the family—*the youngest child who is capable of talking*—asks a leading set of questions about the meaning of Passover.)

We must speak to our children often about our conversion experience and about what the death of Jesus on the cross means to us. Our children should be as familiar with our testimonies as we are. They should know how we regard our lives "before" our acknowledgment of Jesus as Savior and Lord and "after." They should hear us tell of the power of the Lord—His strong hand—that delivered us from evil's bondage and set us toward a land of promise.

What is the purpose? It isn't to build our faith. It isn't so that we might toot our own horns or justify ourselves. No —it is to build up the faith of our children. We rehearse before our children the origin of our relationship with Jesus so that we might establish in them an understanding at a very personal and foundational level the fact that our Lord saves. Our Lord is all-powerful. Our Lord is not only capable of delivering us from evil, but He desires to do so.

In following up their application of blood to the doorposts and lintels of the homes, the Israelites developed a habit of writing a blessing of the Lord and applying it to their homes. Among the words they wrote, and still write today, are Deuteronomy 7:6–8:

> For you are a holy people to the LORD your God; the LORD your God has chosen you to be a people for Himself, a special treasure above all the peoples on the face of the earth. The LORD did not set His love on you nor choose you because you were more in number than any other people, for you were the least of all peoples; but because the LORD loves you, and because He would keep the oath which He swore to your fathers, the LORD has brought you out with a mighty hand, and redeemed you from the house of bondage, from the hand of Pharaoh king of Egypt.

What wonderful and powerful words these are!

In terms of Christ's Passover for you, you, too, are admonished to tell your children that

• God has chosen your children. God intends for them to be among His people. Your children, too, are "special treasures" in God's eyes.

• God loves your children *first,* with an unconditional love. Assure them that God loved them even before you did! God does not love your children because of good behavior or cute dimples or school accomplishments. God loves your children with an endless, boundless love that is separate from what your children do or say. He has chosen your children based on that love, not on their personalities, skills, talents, or accomplishments.

• God is faithful to His promises. He never breaks an oath. He will do what He has promised to your children in His Word.

• God sets us free from bondage. His power is not limited. He is capable of delivering your children from whatever Satan does in an attempt to hold them back, tie them down, or trip them up.

44

God's choosing of your children, His love, His faithfulness, His redemption acts—all are made possible in your children's lives because the blood of Jesus has been applied to your household, a household of faith in Him.

There's no greater message we can share with our children. It is the very cornerstone of their having a sense of value, purpose, and spiritual destiny.

Applying the Lessons of Passover to Your Family

What a wonderful lesson we find in the Passover for the challenge before us as parents. I encourage you today to . . .

• recognize that Jesus died on the cross for your children as well as for you. He included them among those for whom His blood was shed.

• recognize that *your* acceptance of the sacrifice of Jesus extends to, and must be applied to, your family.

• recognize that children are invited to be full partakers in the feast of the Lord. They are to be fed with spiritual food that provides sin-free nourishment for their souls. They are to become keenly aware of their world and their role in the world as salt, light, and speakers of God's Word.

• recognize that children are fellow travelers on the road of faith. They are not to be shunted to one side or left behind. Indeed, the journey is for their sake, and it is to be taken at their pace.

• remind your children with regularity of all that Jesus has done for them. Remind them of God's love for them, of their chosen state before the Lord, and of God's provision for them to deliver them from evil.

Family Principle 6:
God Desires That Families Be Saved Under the New Covenant, Too

Household salvation is not a concept limited to the old covenant, or the Old Testament. It is also evident in the New Testament. It is part of God's plan for fulfilling the covenant established through the death of His Son, Jesus Christ.

Let me point out to you just a few of the instances in the New Testament that refer to the spiritual rebirth of entire households or families.

Zaccheus When Jesus called to Zaccheus and said, "Make haste and come down, for today I must stay at your house," Zaccheus received Him "joyfully." During Jesus' visit with him, Zaccheus stood and said to the Lord, "I give half of my goods to the poor; and if I have taken anything from anyone by false accusation, I restore four-fold." And Jesus said to him, "Today salvation has come to this house, because he also is a son of Abraham; for the Son of Man has come to seek and to save that which was lost." (See Luke 19:1-10.)

Note that Jesus did not say, "Today salvation has come to Zaccheus." He said salvation had come to the house of Zaccheus, referring to his entire family.

Cornelius The devout alms-giving Gentile Cornelius—a centurion of the Italian Regiment—had a vision from God and was told by the Lord to send to Joppa for Simon Peter. The next day, Peter had a vision while he was praying, and the Lord told him, "What God has cleansed you must not call common." As Peter pondered the vision, the men from Cornelius's house arrived and asked Peter to return with them to the house of Cornelius, something Peter, as a righteous Jew, would never have done without such a strong word from the Lord.

When he arrived, Peter found that Cornelius had gathered together "his relatives and close friends." As Peter preached to them, the Holy Spirit fell upon them, and Peter immediately commanded that they be baptized in the name of the Lord. That was the beginning of the spread of Christianity to the gentile world, and it happened within the context of an entire family coming to the Lord! (See Acts 10.)

Lydia   Paul and Silas were staying in Philippi. They went out of the city to a riverside area on the Sabbath day, and there they met with some women who were praying. One of the women, Lydia, was converted, and "she and her household were baptized." The Philippian church was born that day, in the context of an entire family coming to know the Lord. That church was to be one of the powerhouses for the Word of God in all of Macedonia, a church that Paul would later refer to as "my beloved and longed-for brethren, my joy and crown." (See Acts 16:11–15; Phil. 4:1.)

The Philippian jailer   While in Philippi, Paul cast a spirit of divination out of a slave girl, and her masters became so angry when they realized they could no longer use her for economic gain that they seized Paul and Silas and dragged them to the authorities. The magistrates ordered that they be beaten with rods and then thrown into prison.

At midnight, while the two men were singing hymns to the Lord, a great earthquake loosed their chains and opened the doors of the prison. The jailer in charge of their imprisonment awoke, and seeing the door of the jail cell open, he immediately thought that his prisoners had escaped, a very grave matter. He was about to kill himself when Paul called to him, "We are all here." He came to Paul and Silas in trembling and asked, "What must I do to be saved?" The Word of God tells us that Paul responded, "Believe on the Lord Jesus Christ, and you will be saved, you and your household."

Paul and Silas preached the gospel that night to all who were in the jailer's house, and they in turn washed the wounds of the two men. The story concludes this way: "And immediately he and all his family were baptized. Now when he had brought them into his house, he set food before them; and he rejoiced, having believed in God with all his household." (See Acts 16:25–34.)

Other early Christian households   In recounting his ministry among the Corinthians, Paul wrote that he had "also baptized the household of Stephanas" (1 Cor. 1:16). In sending greetings as part of his second letter to Timothy, Paul wrote, "Greet Prisca and Aquila, and the household of Onesiphorus" (2 Tim. 4:19).

The pattern was not for individuals to come to the Lord Jesus but for *households* to come.

The concept ultimately is one of the family of God—or the household of faith—of which all Christians are a part. We are expected as a church to operate as a body but also as a family, with elders and brothers and sisters. We are commissioned by the Lord to bear spiritual children and to nurture them in a family atmosphere of believers.

God's Desire Is for the Entire Family to Know Him

You may ask, "But what of the words of Jesus, then, that His ministry would divide households? For example, in Luke 12:51–53 Jesus is quoted as saying, 'Do you suppose that I came to give peace on earth? I tell you, not at all, but rather division. For from now on five in one house will be divided: three against two, and two against three. Father will be divided against son and son against father, mother against daughter and daughter against mother, mother-in-law against her daughter-in-law and daughter-in-law against her mother-in-law.' "

Jesus is predicting here what will happen as the result

of the human heart, *not* what is desired by the heart of the Lord! Humanity's rebellion and failure to accept the Lord cause a household to be divided. God's earnest desire is that an entire household be saved and serve Him.

Family Principle 7:
God Established His Feasts to
Be Family Events

In the Old Testament, the Lord established several feasts other than Passover as a way of commemorating spiritual events and of passing on their meaning to children. I'll mention two of them.

• The Feast of Tabernacles, including the Feast of Ingathering, was a week of harvest celebration. It was always intended to be a *family* festival. Even today, entire families move into temporary dwellings to commemorate the forty years when the Israelites wandered in the wilderness. This feast is a living story to Jewish children. Children are not taught about the feast or about their heritage. They are invited to relive it and to participate in it.

• The Sabbath, too, was intended to be primarily a *family* feast day and a *family* day of rest in the Lord. Jewish fathers would return home from synagogue, bringing the presence and power of the Lord into their families, where the candles were lighted at sundown and the Sabbath meal was eaten in celebration of the coming day of recreation. Even today, the foremost spiritual celebration of the Jewish faith is the celebration of *Shabbat*—the Sabbath—and the focus for that celebration is the family dinner table.

In the New Testament, this concept of family participation of feasts continued with the Lord's Supper. Throughout the New Testament, we see this as the "table" where believers of all ages, races, and socioeconomic backgrounds are invited to partake of the body and blood of the Lord Jesus Christ.

Are you aware that the Bible does not set an age when a child might first partake of Communion or go to the altar rail to worship God?

We have so laden the Communion service with our traditions that we sometimes lose sight of the fact that children, from the earliest times, were invited to be present to worship the Lord in *all* celebrations of the church.

Children were a part of the first praise and worship services held by the church.

Children heard Paul and John and Peter preach.

Children were witnesses to the miracles wrought by the apostles during the first century.

Children were among the first martyrs.

Children were counted among the first saints.

Both the Old Testament and the New Testament feasts are a means of preparing us for the greatest feast, the one we will enjoy in heaven someday. All of our spiritual family experiences are a means of preparing us to live with the Lord and our fellow Christian believers in eternity, and to live with them *as a family.*

From that perspective, then, we must conclude . . .

Our Homes Are to Be a Reflection of Heaven

Our homes are intended to be a reflection of heaven.

Many parents, however, see their homes as disaster areas, nearly the antithesis of heaven. That isn't what God intended. God intended for your home to be

- a place of peace.
- a place of praise.
- a place of order.

If it isn't, you need to go to the Word of God to rectify the situation.

Our homes are to be a bit of heaven on earth—a place where the will of heaven has been established on this earth.

The father of a family is the embodiment of God to his children. The mother, as she communicates with the father, reflects to the children the role of the church—the full body of believers. The father, as he relates to the mother, reflects the loving, protective, nurturing relationship that God desires for His church.

The local church body, acting in concert with the mother and father, rounds out the rest of the children's image about the way a community of faith should operate.

That's God's plan. It's been His plan from the very foundation of the world.

Either your home will be a seedbed for Godlike faith and Godlike behavior, or it will be a seedbed in which the weeds of a sin nature are allowed to grow unchecked. Furthermore, by your nature you bring sin into your home, but by your faith you lock the destroyer out of your home.

The conclusion is a sobering one when we look into the cribs and the eyes of our children:

Our family life is the greatest determiner
of our children's spiritual future.

4

Embracing What God Requires of You as a Parent

Come, you children, listen to me;
I will teach you the fear of the LORD.
—Psalm 34:11

Let me tell you the true story of two little boys. Both of them were part of the same church. One Sunday, fliers were distributed to the parents about a Christian camp, and one boy's parents decided to send him. The camp featured far more than fun and games. Every day, the children were invited to enter into praise and worship. The Word of God was preached with power to those young people. They were invited to accept the Lord Jesus Christ into their lives as their personal Savior and Lord. And they were challenged to live holy Christ-honoring lives. Nobody said to the children, "You're too young to experience the Lord," or "You're not capable of living a Christian life." The little boy who went to the camp came home having invited Jesus into his life, and having made a strong commitment to serve the Lord.

Several days after the boy's return home, his friend invited him to go to a movie with a group of boys. He asked, "What are you going to see?"

When he heard the name of the movie, he responded, "I don't think it would be pleasing to Jesus for me to see that movie." His friend, of course, was a bit dumbfounded by that response, but the boy stood firm by his decision: "I can't go to the movie with you. I don't think it would be the right thing to do." The second boy went to the movie without him.

During the show, one of the boys in the group passed a butane lighter down the aisle and dared the other boys to sniff it to get high. The second little boy did and passed out instantly. He was dead by the time they got him to the hospital.

The pastor who told me this story said, "That was the saddest funeral I have ever preached. We parents never think that we might bury our children. If we were more aware of all the dangers facing our children today, we'd probably take far more seriously their need to make a decision for the Lord *as children.*"

The Lord requires us to take seriously the need for our children to make decisions for Him and to live for Him, *and* He requires us to *prepare* our children for making that decision.

First and foremost, however, God calls us as Christian parents to be "surety" for our children.

Becoming "Surety" for Your Children

We learn something about surety from the book of Genesis:

> Then Judah said to Israel his father, "Send the lad with me, and we will arise and go, that we may live and not die, both we and you and also our little ones. I myself will be surety for him; from my hand you shall require him. If I do not bring him back to you and set him before you, then let me bear the blame forever" (43:8–9).

This prayer should be spoken by every married couple before they ever conceive a child or by every couple that already has a child.

What does it mean to be surety? It means that you place your life as collateral for your children.

When you go to the bank and get a credit card with which to charge purchases, you have put into effect a policy of an unsecured loan. The bank gives you a card based on your ability to earn, and it can cancel your card and sue you for any amount that you don't pay. But when you go to the bank to borrow money for a house, that type of loan usually is a secured loan, which means that you have put up some type of collateral to get the loan. The collateral is other real property that indicates you have an ability to earn and to make payments. The collateral is also put at risk to the bank, which means that the bank has the privilege of taking the collateral you have put up as payment should you default on the loan.

In this story of the Bible, the sons of Jacob—also known as Israel—had gone down to Egypt to get food because a severe famine had gripped the land where they were living. Joseph, their brother whom they had sold into slavery many years before, had been elevated to the role of prime minister of Egypt. He was in charge of food distribution. When they came before Joseph to make their request for food, they did not recognize him, but Joseph recognized them. He gave them some food, but he insisted that before he would give them any more food, one of the brothers, Simeon, had to remain behind in Egypt. The rest of the brothers were to return and bring back with them their youngest brother, Benjamin, who was Joseph's full brother.

The brothers were reluctant to do as he asked. They knew that their father, Jacob, had clung to Benjamin as the only remaining son of his beloved wife Rachel after he had been told that Joseph was dead. Still, the famine continued, and to have food to eat, Judah—the leading brother of the family—rose up and said to his father, "Please let Benjamin go with me. I will be 100 percent responsible for his life. If any harm comes to him, the blame will be solely on me, not on you. I will put my own life completely on the line for Benjamin's safe return."

It is a statement of total commitment. And it's the challenge we face as parents.

It's as if the Lord has issued us an invitation that says, "Please come to live with Me for eternity. Bring your children with you." The postscript may well read, "Don't come without them."

Are you willing to risk being surety for your children today? Are you willing to say to your heavenly Father, "Please entrust these children to me on the earth. I will be 100 percent responsible for their spiritual lives. I will be their collateral. If any spiritual harm comes to them, put the blame on me, not them. I will put my entire life on the line to see that my children come to know You. I will be the collateral for my children's lives. If they end up deserving to be punished, send me instead"?

When Judah and Benjamin and the rest of the brothers returned to Egypt and stood before Joseph a second time, Joseph gave them food and sent them on their way, but he had his servants hide his silver cup in the sack of Benjamin's grain. After the brothers had begun their journey home, Joseph said to his steward, "Follow the men and say, 'Why did you repay evil for good? One of you has taken our master's cup.' " When confronted by Joseph's servants, the brothers quickly opened their sacks of grain. When the silver cup was found in Benjamin's sack, they tore their clothes, and they all returned with him to Joseph's city. Joseph said to them, "You all may return home except the one in whose sack my cup was found. He must remain and be my servant."

And Judah spoke up and said, "If we do not return home

with this brother, our father will die in his grief." The Scriptures use these wonderful words to describe the relationship of Jacob with his son Benjamin: "His life is bound up in the lad's life" (Gen. 44:30).

Judah continued,

> Your servant became surety for the lad to my father, saying, "If I do not bring him back to you, then I shall bear the blame before my father forever." Now therefore, please let your servant remain instead of the lad as a slave to my lord, and let the lad go up with his brothers. For how shall I go up to my father if the lad is not with me, lest perhaps I see the evil that would come upon my father?" (Gen. 44:32–34).

Judah gave little thought to himself, his future, his own family. He acted on his statement of surety, to give his own life as collateral for his brother. He then fell on his knees and interceded for the life of his brother, saying, "I would rather give my life to you as a slave than to return home without him."

If the story ended there, it would be a sad story, although one of personal courage and integrity. The story, however, had a good ending. Joseph told his brothers who he was, and he hugged his brothers and wept with them. At first, they were dismayed that the brother they had so mistreated was standing before them, and with such great power over them, but Joseph said to them,

> Do not therefore be grieved or angry with yourselves because you sold me here; for God sent me before you to preserve life. . . . And God sent me before you to preserve a posterity for you in the earth, and to save your lives by a great deliverance. So now it was not you who sent me here, but God; and He has made me a father to

Pharaoh, and lord of all his house, and a ruler throughout all the land of Egypt. (Gen. 45:5, 7–8).

The brothers, including Benjamin, returned to their father and told him all that had happened. Jacob and his entire family moved to Egypt, to the land of Goshen, where they could be near Joseph and have all their needs met.

How does this episode relate to you today as a parent with spiritual responsibility for your children?

First, you are challenged to put your life on the line for the spiritual well-being of your children.

That sounds fairly straightforward and easy in theory. In practice, it is the toughest thing you will ever do.

Being spiritual surety for your children means that you put their spiritual needs before all other needs faced by either your children or yourself. It means a complete reordering of your priorities and those of your entire family.

Putting your children's spiritual development first means that you put it before your job, your career, your own pleasure, your own desires, your own leisure pursuits, your own friends. It means . . .

• when faced with a decision regarding use of time, resources, or behavior, you ask yourself, What is best for my children's spiritual future?

• when you plan your family's activities and set into motion a daily and weekly and annual schedule for your family to keep, you ask, What are we doing for the spiritual welfare of our children?

• when you evaluate your children's toys and playmates, their schooling, their classes at church, you ask, Am I providing the very best I can for the spiritual growth and development of my children?

I am continually amazed at the Christian parents who spend more time taking their children to movies than to church. I am equally amazed at the parents who do a great deal of research about which preschool they should choose for their children but know nothing about what happens to them when they go downstairs for the children's program while parents go upstairs to worship the Lord. I am amazed at the parents who are vitally concerned about providing pure water and air and healthy foods for their children but seem totally unconcerned about what they read or watch on television.

Your number one responsibility as a Christian parent is to train up children who will love and serve the Lord. That is priority number one. All else is a distant second.

The grades your children make in school are not nearly as important as their spiritual development.

The popularity of your children among peers is not nearly as important as their living with you in heaven one day.

The ability of your children to attend a top-rated college, get a high-paying job, and live at the top of the social ladder pales by comparison to their future as spiritual warriors for the Lord.

Making their spiritual growth and development your top concern in life is not automatic, and it certainly isn't easy.

It means turning off the television set and reading with and talking to your children about things that truly matter.

It means taking your free time and lavishing it on your children, developing a relationship with them that has the Lord Jesus Christ at its core.

It means getting home from work early enough to tuck your children into bed with a prayer and a hug.

It means keeping your children at the forefront of your thinking and sacrificing some of your concentration on other areas of your career to be there for your children in critically spiritual moments.

One key phrase that we have heard in the last decade has been that of "quality time." I am a firm believer in quality time. The highest quality of time you can give your children is a time of sharing Jesus with them. In practical terms, that may mean a time of prayer, a time spent reading and discussing God's Word, a time going for a walk and talking about God's world and God's nature, a quiet time of listening to them talk about their dreams and ideas and goals, including their spiritual dreams and visions.

Quality time, however, is not a substitute for "quantity time." You must recognize that some of the most important spiritual moments in each child's life occur on the child's timetable, not yours. To help your child in those moments, you've got to be available. You've got to be in tune, spiritually, with where each child is every day, every week, every month, every year.

You've got to spend enough time with your children to have a full awareness of what is troubling them, what is challenging them, what they are struggling against or coping with. You've got to be in spiritual sync with your children.

Judah didn't know that Jacob loved Benjamin and had his life "bound up in the lad's life" because he had heard a family rumor. Nobody had told him the fact because of a parent-teacher conference. It wasn't a juvenile officer from the local police department who brought him the insight. No, Judah lived in intimate relationship with his brothers and father. He knew from firsthand experience the depth of that relationship.

The only way you can truly know where your children are spiritually is to spend time with them doing and experiencing spiritual things!

Why am I so concerned about time? Because it directly relates to priority. We spend our time doing the things that matter to us most.

Give yourself a time audit as a parent. How do you

spend your day? How much of your time is focused on your children?

Many fathers have said to me, "I work long hours at the office so I can provide for my family. My main time with my children is on weekends."

I often question these fathers further: "What are you trying to provide for your family?"

"Well," they usually respond, "food on the table, clothes, a nice house, a nice car, enough toys, fun vacations and outings."

Occasionally, a parent will respond, "I'm working overtime so my children can attend a Christian school. It's a sacrifice we've all agreed to make as a family." That, however, is rare. Most of the time, the parent responds by listing provisions that are material and have no bearing on eternity or on the spiritual development of the children.

Providing things *for* our children can never be as important as directly providing things *to* our children: our time, our insight, our attention, our effort, our presence.

I came across a study a few years ago that documented the amount of time the average father in our nation spends talking to and listening to each of his children. The figure was astounding to me: under five minutes a day. In fact, the figure was closer to ninety seconds on weekdays.

Out of twenty-four hours, the average father in our nation managed to squeeze out only five minutes for each child? That's about .003 percent of his daily time! What can possibly be accomplished for eternity if that is the average?

The greatest pain of my personal life as an evangelist, who speaks in some 150 different meetings a year, is the amount of time I must be away from my home. I recognize the challenge faced by many parents who must travel as a part of the jobs the Lord has called them to do. What can those of us who are on the road do?

One thing I do is to take my wife and three children with me as much as I possibly can. When I can't take them with me, I talk to each one every day. I send cards to my children—some arrive while I'm away, some while I'm home. Either way, my children have the benefit of knowing that I was and am thinking about them.

And perhaps most important of all, when I am home with my wife and children, I am totally and completely at home with them. No television. No going out unless we can all go together. No distractions allowed. I choose to unplug the phone and simply "be" with those I love more than any other people on this earth.

None of us as parents can ever be with our children *all* of the time. When we are with our children, however, we can give them all of our attention. And we can constantly seek new ways of giving our children more and more of our time.

There's a further action you must take beyond making the spiritual growth of your children your foremost priority in life . . .

Second, you are challenged to intercede for your children before the throne of the Lord Jesus Christ on a daily basis.

The Scriptures tell us that Judah fell on his knees and pleaded with Joseph for the welfare of his brother Benjamin.

When was the last time you fell to your knees and pleaded with the Lord for your children? When was the last time you interceded for your children in prayer?

In praying for your children, you'll be joining such Bible heroes as Abraham, Manoah, David, Job, the father of a demoniac boy, Jairus, and the mother of a sick daughter. (See Gen. 17:18, 20; Judg. 13:8; 2 Sam. 12:16; Job 1:5; Matt. 17:15; Mark 5:23; 7:26.)

The very word *intercede,* by definition, has an element of begging or pleading to it. An intercessor is a mediator who stands between two parties, begging to one for the welfare of the other.

You must realize that you can't do it all for your children. You can't know it all . . . be it all . . . have it all . . . provide it all . . . arrange it all . . . purchase it all . . . give it all . . . or cover it all. You can do a great deal for your children in arranging the environment in which they grow up and in expressing to them the fullness of your own faith. But when it comes right down to it, you can't do everything.

You can't be with your children twenty-four hours a day. You can't watch over and protect your children in all situations. You can't stand guard over everything your children take into their minds or bodies. You can't mediate the influence of all other people on their lives.

And ultimately, you can't save your children. Only the Lord Jesus Christ can do that through His shed blood on the cross. No matter how much you give, even to the point of dying for your children, you cannot *make* your children choose the Lord.

At first reading, this comment may seem to contradict what I have said earlier about household salvation. It doesn't. As a parent, you can walk with your children all the way along the path from their birth right up to the foot of the cross. You can sing praises with them, pray with them, teach them, talk with them about the Lord, train them in spiritual practices, and dance with the joy of the Lord all the way to the foot of the cross. Indeed, that is what you *must* do as a Christian parent. You must prepare your children as best you possibly can for a life of faith and Christian service. But once you arrive at the foot of the cross and the children face the decision of choosing or refusing Jesus as their Savior, each child's decision will be the *child's* decision. You can't get up on the cross and die for them.

That realization puts you in a pleading and begging position before the Lord. You must cry out to the Lord on behalf of your children.

Every night that I am home, I go into my children's rooms after they have gone to sleep, and I pray over them this one main prayer: that the presence of God will be made real to them. I pray many other things, of course, for them, but this is my one abiding and overriding prayer. If the presence of God is real to them, they will never want to be *out* of His presence.

What else do you plead for?

• You beg the Lord to have mercy upon your children.

• You beg the Lord to exert the full influence of the Holy Spirit upon your children.

• You beg the Lord to watch over your children continually and to keep them safe and healthy and protected from all natural and spiritual harm.

• You beg the Lord to send His angels to guard the footsteps of your children.

• You beg the Lord to provide the best possible friends, teachers, peers, mentors and, one day, spouses for your children.

• You beg the Lord to send godly men and women to teach your children in Sunday school and at church youth events.

• You beg the Lord to blind your children's eyes to evil, and to keep them from hearing, seeing, or otherwise partaking of those things that might destroy their innocence or bring about their destruction.

Intercession is not a polite, quiet, casual form of prayerful communication with the Lord. Intercession is intense. It's praying as if life itself is at stake—which is the real truth of the matter. Your children's eternal lives *are* at stake. It's praying with the intent that you will not get up from your knees unless and until you feel a release in your spirit. It's praying with faith that God hears your prayer and that you are praying in the will of heaven so that God will answer your prayer. Intercession is praying with such intensity that you sense you just may die in the process; what you are praying for is so dear, so important, so critical to you that you are willing to give your very life to see your prayer answered.

Let me ask you again, "When was the last time you interceded in prayer for your children's spiritual future?"

Third, the Lord requires that you intentionally seek to pass your faith to your children to prepare them for lives of service to Him.

Not only do I pass my natural physical traits to my children, I also pass to them my redemption and the grace extended to me by the Lord Jesus Christ.

Consider the pregnant woman. The child growing in her womb does not eat on his own. The child's nutrition is directly based on what the mother eats. Food is passed through the placenta to the child.

Is the child in the womb an independent human being? In many ways, the answer must be yes. The child has a unique genetic code, a unique personality and set of physical traits already under development. In other ways, the answer must be no. The child draws from and benefits from the nature of the mother. The mother's physical and emotional health has a direct bearing on the child's growth and development. The womb is more than just an environment. It is a life-sustaining environment and, even more, an environment that makes life possible.

The same is true in the spiritual sense. Your children are born as individual human beings with their own free will and personalities—and their own direct relationship with the heavenly Father. At the same time, they are placed in the spiritual womb of your home where they are under spiritual protection and nourishment that have a direct bearing on their spiritual life and development.

The spirit of the adults in the family communicates to the children in much the same way that the nutrients ingested by a mother are passed along to the child inside her.

Have you ever danced with a child by placing the child's feet on your own feet? Perhaps you've walked with your child in that manner, placing his feet on yours and holding him by his hands, moving one step at a time. The child's moves mirror your own. It's as if your child is dancing or walking, and yet the moves your child is making are not solely his own.

This is yet another way of looking at the spiritual relationship between parent and children. Your role as a parent is to dance or to walk your children into the throne room of the Lord, right up to Jesus, and then just one step away from Him, you stop and let your children take that final step into His arms.

From the foundation of the world, the Lord has desired that your children would be godly seed on this earth. God's vote for your children has already been cast.

If you, as a Christian parent, desire your children to grow up to love and serve the Lord and to live with you forever in a heavenly home . . .

And if the church community in which your "home" is embedded is also ardent in its desire that your children love the Lord with all their hearts, minds, and souls . . .

Circumstances favor your children not only accepting Jesus as their personal Savior and Lord but also loving and serving the Lord every day of their lives.

And that's the way God intended it.

He didn't intend for children to flounder or be ungrounded.

He didn't intend for children to be spiritually barren until some magical age of accountability.

He didn't intend for children to grow up without spiritual roots and then develop those roots as adults.

Nothing in His Word even hints that these are the desires of God.

Rather, God's desire is that your children be rooted and grounded in the faith . . . that they have a rich spiritual life at every stage of development . . . and that they put down deep spiritual roots that become firmly entrenched and not easily shaken.

To that end, the Lord has called you as a parent to be the priest of the home and the minister of the home.

What is the difference?

A priest joins God and human. A minister equips.

The priestly function is one of linking the divine with the human—of connecting God with your children and your children with God.

A minister functions to provide for others what they need to grow in their knowledge and love of God or what they need in order to do what God has called them to do. Your children need to hear the Word of the Lord and to hear how to apply that Word on a daily basis.

Fourth, the Lord challenges you to talk about Him on a daily basis in your home.

One of the most famous admonitions related to child rearing in the entire Bible is this:

> Hear, O Israel: The LORD our God, the LORD is one! You shall love the LORD your God with all your heart, with all your soul, and with all your might. And these words which I command you today shall be in your heart. You shall teach them diligently to your children, and shall talk of them when you sit in your house, when you walk by the way, when you lie down, and when you rise up. You shall bind

them as a sign on your hand, and they shall be as frontlets between your eyes. You shall write them on the doorposts of your house and on your gates (Deut. 6:4–9).

This passage in Deuteronomy admonishes you to talk the Word to your children. It doesn't say to read the Bible to them in a formal way. It doesn't say to lead them in formal prayer sessions. It says to talk to your children in the morning, noon, and evening—everywhere you go—about the Lord.

You may say, "I don't know the Bible that well."

What *do* you know about the Lord? What *do* you know of God's Word? Share that!

Your obligation is to tell your children everything you know about Him and about His Word. Even if you feel that you know only a little, share that!

Don't put yourself under a burden to teach your children the Bible. Learn the Bible for yourself. Be a student of the Word. Study it on your own. Grow in your knowledge of the world. And out of what you learn, talk to your children. Share the insights you discover as a natural part of your daily conversation.

When I was a child, my father traveled extensively as an evangelist. But my father was not like many evangelists who preach only a handful of sermons. He continually developed new sermons, and guess who he used as his audience for rehearsal? Even when I was three years old, my father practiced his sermons on me as we went for walks. He did it in a natural, conversational way. Only later did I realize that what we talked about in the car on our way to a city was what I was going to hear in sermon form that night. My father's spiritual growth was pumped into me, and I absorbed it as best I could as a child.

What do you talk about in your family? Is it Nintendo? Is it gossip about other people? Is it sports? Some children know more about baseball stars than about the Lord

Jesus. Consider your family topics of conversation. The foremost one should be of the things of the Lord.

In sum . . .

The Lord challenges you

• to make the Lord's work the priority of your home and to sacrifice your will for the spiritual growth and nurture of your children.

• to intercede for your children, diligently and regularly.

• to accept God's call to pass your faith to your children and to make a commitment to do so.

• to talk about the things of the Lord in your home on a daily basis.

In many ways, these four responsibilities embody the same principles of ministry leadership set forth for the church by the apostle Paul: "And He Himself gave some to be apostles, some prophets, some evangelists, and some pastors and teachers, for the equipping of the saints for the work of ministry, for the edifying of the body of Christ" (Eph. 4:11–12).

If, indeed, your home is a microcosm of the kingdom of God to your children . . .

And if as the leader of your home, you are called by God to be a priest and a minister over your home . . .

These callings apply to you, too!

The Lord calls you to be an apostle to your children
God intends for you to blaze a trail for your children—to give them a vision of what they might be in the Lord and accomplish for the Lord and, above all, to give your children an awareness that God has a unique plan and purpose for their lives. How can you be an apostle to your children? By teaching them to trust God to reveal His will in their lives—to seek it, ask for it, and look for it daily.

The Lord calls you to be a priest to your children As already stated, God intends for you to intercede for your children and to teach them how to develop a loving, intimate relationship with the Father.

You are a priest to your children when you pray for them daily, let them hear you pray for them often, and teach them to talk to God daily for themselves.

The Lord calls you to be a prophet to your children God intends for you to proclaim the Word of the Lord to your children and to portray for them their future in the Lord.

How can you be a prophet to your children?

First, by pointing out examples every day of the Lord at work.

Second, by expressing to them their future in the Lord. Talk about

• *heaven.* Paint for your children a vivid picture of eternal life. Talk about all of the wonderful things that will be in heaven and all of the things that won't be there that your children will be happy to do without!

• *a godly life.* Paint for your children a vivid picture of a life that embodies the teachings of Jesus, a life of service to others.

• *evangelism.* Give your children a vivid picture of *their* winning souls.

The Lord calls you to be a teacher to your children God intends for you to be the primary teacher of His Word to your children.

How can you be a Bible teacher to your children?

Encourage them to read the Bible.

Encourage the memorization of Scripture verses.

Talk about the Word of God as you come and go. Point out examples to your children of Bible-based consequences. (We'll discuss this further in chapter 8.)

The Lord calls you to be an evangelist to your children
God intends for you to be the primary voice sharing with your children the facts about Jesus Christ: His birth, life, death on the cross, resurrection from the dead, and ascension into heaven, where He can be found today, seated at the right hand of the Father, interceding on our behalf.

How can you be an evangelist to your children?

Talk about Jesus. Tell the stories about the life of Jesus. Tell what His death and resurrection mean.

Talk about God's plan for salvation and the importance of receiving Jesus into one's life.

If someone asks you if you are involved in ministry, say, "Yes! I'm a Christian parent." In fact, you can truthfully say, "I'm involved in ministry twenty-four hours a day!"

God will not usurp your position as a parent. Neither will He do your job for you. He requires of you as a parent to be His minister in your home.

What About the Single Parent?

If you are a single parent, you have an especially tough challenge in training your children. Nevertheless, the Lord promises to be a spouse to you and a father to your children. Trust Him to give you the wisdom you need to fill both father and mother roles.

If you have an ungodly spouse, you are in the same position as a single parent. Trust the Lord to honor what you do and say for Him.

Do you remember the journey of Moses and his wife, Zipporah, and their children on the way from the wilderness to the courts of Pharaoh? The Lord stopped Moses on that journey and threatened to take his life because Moses had not circumcised his son. In other words, Moses had not done what was required by God's law for his children truly to be counted as godly seed of the house of Israel. (See Exod. 4:24–26.)

Zipporah, his wife, took a sharp stone and cut the foreskin of her son. She was not happy about doing it. Still, she realized that she had no choice in the matter. For God's full blessing to be on her family, her child needed to be a full member of the chosen people of God.

Zipporah was in a position that she was never created to take on. God had called the man to be the priest of his home. But there her husband was, sick unto death. And Zipporah was forced into the role of family priest.

If you are a single parent today, or the wife of a husband who is not fulfilling the priestly role in your family, you are in Zipporah's position. Ask the Lord to give you the courage and wisdom to be the priest of your home and to do what is necessary for training your children to be part of God's chosen seed on this earth.

What About the Children's Choice?

I have a firm belief that if we make enough quality decisions for our children when they are too young to make decisions for themselves, they will have a difficult time making poor decisions when they *do* reach the age of making decisions.

I have talked with many parents through the years who have made statements such as these to me:

• "Well, I'm going to wait until my child is older, and then I'm going to let him decide for himself what he wants to do about God and about going to church."

• "My parents thrust religion down my throat, and I'm not going to do that to my child. When she's older, I'll tell her what I believe and give her the option of deciding to follow Jesus or not."

• "My child has free will just as I do. It's not up to me to force my child into believing any one thing."

I categorically reject these lines of thinking. In the first place, children who are not trained up in the faith are children left to flounder spiritually.

These same parents would never dream of letting their children potty train themselves whenever and however they felt like it. They would never say, "I'm going to let my child decide when he reaches his teen years how he feels about wearing clothes or about brushing his teeth." Why do they automatically assume that the spiritual growth and development of children are anything other than a training process?

Second, I'd like to point out that I'm not talking about "religion." I'm talking about a relationship in which God is our heavenly Father; Jesus is our Savior, Lord, and older brother in the family of God; and the Holy Spirit is our ever-present comforter and counselor. Relationships are built through association. They are based on communication and familiarity, not ritual or dogma.

The parents who say, "I'll let my children decide how they feel about the heavenly Father when they become adults," probably would *not* say, "I don't think I'll expose my children to any of their grandparents, aunts, or uncles. I'll let them decide whether they want to be related to those people when they reach puberty." The fact is, the children *are* related to their grandparents, aunts or uncles, and cousins whether they think they are, choose to be, or desire to be.

The spiritual analogy is a strong one. Your children are related to God the Father because you are. They will develop either a good relationship with the heavenly Father or a poor one, but nonetheless, a relationship exists because of your spiritual commitment.

Finally, children do not have totally free will. None of us

does. Our will is hemmed in and focused at an early age in very practical ways. Johnny isn't allowed to bash in Susie's head with a toy, even though he may "will" to do so. Susie isn't allowed to throw food at Johnny even though she feels "free" to exert her will in that way.

The same holds true for the spiritual will of children. The will must be trained and directed toward behavior that is deemed acceptable by the community at large. To the Christian parent and family, that community at large is the church. Acceptable behavior toward God is usually behavior regarded as reverent, trusting, and obedient. Acceptable behavior toward others in the church is usually that regarded as kind, giving, longsuffering, patient, edifying, and helpful. It is a parent's spiritual responsibility to nurture these qualities in children and to help children channel the will into activities and behaviors that reflect the norms of the larger spiritual community.

In sum, children who are born into a strong household faith, and who are trained up to do good works and reflect loving behavior toward both God and humankind, are children who do not have much of a choice. Praying parents have predetermined that the children will grow up within the body of Christ.

Consider for a moment children born in America. They are born with a certain predetermined destiny—to live in a land of political freedom, to receive an education (as prescribed by law), and to obey the laws of the land.

We do not say about our newborns, "I wonder if they'll want to be citizens of the United States when they grow up?" On the contrary. Children born on U.S. soil are regarded as United States citizens even if neither parent is a citizen! Neither do we say, "We'll make freedom and education and obedience to laws available as optional behaviors to our children as they reach an age when they understand those concepts." Our children grow up knowing they *are* free, they *must* go to school, and they are *required* to obey the nation's laws or face punitive consequences.

Why would Christian parents assume anything less for the children? The children born to us are not only born into a political nation; they are born into the church. The norms of the church that we value highly—those aspects of faith and behavior (or works)—must also be the norms of our homes.

Consider, too, the aspects of culture and race as predetermining factors for our children. Every child is born into a culture and into a race of people. Identity as the member of a certain race or culture is determined without any choice or input on the child's part. I was born to parents of English and Germanic ancestry. I cannot change that bloodline. I am Caucasian. I spent many of my growing-up years in southern California. Many influences of the culture in which I was raised were givens. I couldn't have escaped them had I tried. I attended schools that operated according to a certain educational philosophy. I grew up in a neighborhood that was structured in a certain way. Freeways and shopping centers and a sprawling city life were givens. All of those aspects of my culture and race had an influence on my life apart from any decision I made as a child.

J. H. Jowett put it this way in his book *The Eagle Life:*

Now, what does every generation teach to its successor? It teaches its language, its laws, its customs. It preserves by instinctive action the continuity of national existence. And it teaches more. Every generation, whether it thinks that it is doing so or not, is communicating its own morals to the generation that is springing up, imparting its own ideas, conveying by all manner of subtle but very effective means its estimate of things, its sentiments, its convictions, or its want of convictions. And all this works automatically.

The spiritual identity of children is also affected by the spiritual culture or heritage of the community into which they are born. What parents believe about God and how a family is structured in relationship to the church greatly affect the development of children's spiritual nature— even if the parents are not intentional about what they are doing, and regardless of what the children may desire.

Let me give you a couple of examples. Billy is born into a home in which both parents have a strong personal faith. The family prays openly at mealtimes and bedtimes, and in times of crisis—such as scraped knees or playground conflicts—prayer is a first course of action. On Sundays, the family attends church and Sunday school. Only severe family illness keeps the family from attending. On Wednesday evenings, the family participates in a small Bible study fellowship group from the church. Jesus is talked about openly and regularly. Praise music rather than pop music is played in the home. Family decisions are based on a strong Christian ethic. Billy is in a decidedly Christ-centered environment. His culture has been established for him.

Clarence, on the other hand, is growing up in a family in which both parents claim to be Christians. They bow for a moment of silence before meals, and that is virtually the extent of a daily acknowledgment of God. They attend church on Sundays when the weather and soccer schedules permit. If a serious moral problem arises, they might consult a minister. Clarence is in an environment that has been established for him.

To say that Billy's environment has stripped away his spiritual free will and Clarence's environment allows for free will is inaccurate. Both environments have been predetermined by their parents. Both boys are being trained up with a certain perspective toward God. Both will be products of their upbringings. Neither has a choice about the family culture in which he finds himself. Both will have a choice later in life about how they want to raise their own children—but only to an extent. The greater likelihood is that they will perpetuate the pattern of their childhoods in the lives of their children.

Do your children have a choice?

Not really.

The true biblical pattern is closer to this:

> *You raise your children to choose the relationship with God that you have chosen for them.*

Is This Brainwashing?

When I was a guest on "The Sally Jessy Raphael Show," the founder of the League to Abolish Religion in America heard me share this viewpoint and accused me of promoting the brainwashing of children. Believe me, I was sorely offended.

Granted, our children need their minds washed by the Word of God. But brainwashing is not what happens when we share the Word of God with our children in an intentional, conscientious, daily way.

Brainwashing is a technique that couples repetition and torture (physical or emotional) to get persons to adhere to a belief they otherwise would not hold. Brainwashing involves the association of pain with a message. That's the exact opposite of what we are doing when we cultivate a love for the Lord in our children's lives.

We as Christian parents must never use pain to demand that our children believe in the Lord. We must never associate the gospel message with a threat of torture. If we do so, the good news ceases to be good news!

The gospel frees persons to fulfill their potential in Christ. It brings a freedom of spirit and joy. It provides for the release of guilt. It separates from death-causing, pain-producing sin.

When we daily, repetitively share the Word of the Lord with our children, we build them up, not tear them down. We train them for a life of blessing.

Your children are going to follow somebody's thoughts. That's just the way human nature operates. Children see and copy. They learn how to behave and what to believe from somebody.

If you abdicate that responsibility out of a fear that you will be unduly manipulating or brainwashing your children, you must face the fact that you are not leaving your children as blank slates. You are handing their minds and hearts over to someone else and giving that person the privilege of writing a message on your children's lives.

If your children do not follow in your footsteps to love and serve the Lord, they will follow in the footsteps of somebody at some time in life, and it likely will be a set of footsteps that does *not* lead to heaven.

A Deeper Level of Commitment

Making this level of commitment to your children—to make their spiritual growth and development your top priority in life, to intercede frequently for them, to model Christian faith and behavior for them, to talk to them daily about the things of the Lord—is a deeper commitment than most Christian parents have made.

Many parents have stood at an altar or baptismal font and have dedicated their children to the Lord or have made a profession of faith as part of an infant baptism ceremony. They might have truly meant their dedication vows to raise up their children in a Christian home and to keep them involved in a church.

I've never witnessed a baby dedication or infant baptism service, however, in which the parents were challenged to make the child's spiritual growth their top priority in life, to intercede for the spiritual well-being of the child, or to express daily to the child the Word of the Lord —at least not in such clearly expressed terms. It is my experience that unless you are really sure about what you are signing on to do—whether it's in a job assignment or parenting—you tend to fail or to fall short.

Let me make the challenge to you today in vow form.

• Will you as a parent make a vow today to put your children's spiritual formation—spiritual growth and development—as the top priority of your life?

• Will you as a parent make a vow today to readjust your family schedule to provide the spiritual nourishment and activities that your children need?

• Will you as a parent make a vow today to intercede in prayer before the Lord for the spiritual well-being and future of your children?

• Will you vow to present your children with a living faith—one you walk daily and talk about daily with your children?

There's a certificate at the back of this book that you may want to sign and date as a living pledge to your children if you are willing to make that vow today. I pray that you will. In the process, I assure you that your life as you presently know it will be changed. I also give you this word of promise—the lives of your children will be changed for eternity.

5

Displaying God's Nature
to Your Children

His descendants will be mighty on earth;
The generation of the upright will be blessed.
—*Psalm 112:2*

A mother elephant carries her baby twenty-two months before it is born, and twenty-two months after its birth, that baby elephant is fully grown.

Can you imagine having a baby and, two years later, seeing that child fully grown and playing football for the Browns?

Twenty-four hours after a guinea pig is born, it can live independently of its mother. It is born with its eyes open, ready to move around, and a day later, it is eating solid food.

Can you imagine giving birth to a child and, a day later, having it be able to walk and feed itself?

God designed the human reproductive process to be one of slow maturation and development. Why? I believe He knew that it would take years for us to instill in our children the spiritual principles that they would need to live successful adult Christian lives—principles that are eternal and designed to prepare a living human being for eternity.

Physical growth happens rapidly elsewhere in the natural world. Even mental growth can happen far faster than spiritual or emotional development. (Children can recite facts and figures far quicker than they can grasp their meaning or application within a context of moral values. They can decipher problems and come up with "right answers" long before they are able to live out right from wrong.)

Spiritual growth and maturation take time, and that fact, in my opinion, is the primary reason for the establishment of the family.

I like the way Floyd McClung, Jr., expressed this idea in his book *The Father Heart of God:*

> God designed us to begin our lives as babies, totally dependent and vulnerable, because He intended the family to be the setting in which His love was modeled so that children would grow up feeling understood, loved, and accepted. Nurtured in this kind of loving, secure environment, youngsters could develop a healthy, God-based self-esteem and see themselves as wanted, important, valuable, and good.

Mother and father animals rarely stick by their offspring very long. They don't need to. They can model all of the behavior that their baby animals need to learn in a matter of days, weeks, or months. What they don't model is passed on through instincts. Human mothers and fathers, however, *must* stick by their offspring. It's as if the physical maturation process has been slowed for us human beings so that we will have ample time to instill principles vital for spiritual maturation.

This very process of slow growth allows us as parents to present before our children perhaps the most basic of God's attributes—His longsuffering loyalty to us. God is committed to us not for a day or a year but for a lifetime.

God does not create us and then push us out of His nest. No, He nurtures. He builds us up slowly. He walks with us through life. From conception until the day of our death, He is with us and ever working on our behalf—because He is preparing us to live with Him forever.

As parents, we are compelled by the Lord to model these same attributes to our children. We do so primarily through *emotional* means.

Most of us think of teaching and learning as processes involving the mind, and they are. The process of teaching your children the nature of the Lord is not one of teaching as much as a process of *instilling*. It is a process rooted in emotion.

You Hold the Key to Your Children's Hearts

A child's first and most basic way of dealing with her world is through emotions. A child is born with an amazing ability to perceive emotionally, to be sensitive to the feelings of others. Watch a child nestle into the bosom of a mother who dearly loves her, wants her, and is at peace with the world. Contrast that to a newborn who is handed to a mother filled with anger, resentment, and frustration.

Children remain extremely sensitive to emotions during the first five years of their lives. What does that mean to us as Christian parents? It means that our primary way of communicating our spiritual life to our children is through emotional means—hugging, touching, cuddling, being close, holding, gently caressing, tenderly kissing.

The most attractive emotion to children is the one that attracts adults: love. Children respond to love. They blossom under it. It modifies their behavior and their character in a way that is far more potent than giving them information or a lush, beautiful, secure physical environment.

In other words, what we tell our children about God and

His love is not nearly as important as what we show our children about God and His love. They can comprehend God's love only if they first feel our love.

One of the most interesting studies along this line was published by Stella Chess and Alexander Thomas in their book *Temperament and Behavior Disorder in Children.* Chess and Thomas identified temperaments in newborns considered to be basic characteristics of children, ones that stay with them all their lives. They include activity level, rhythmicity, approach or withdrawal, adaptability, intensity of reaction, threshold of responsiveness, quality of mood, distractibility, attention span, and persistence. Chess and Thomas concluded that these basic characteristics are directly related to the type of mothering and nurturing children receive in this way: The stronger the love bond and the greater the amount of nurturing received, the more children can *grow* in each characteristic.

A thirty-six-year study conducted by David C. McClelland and Joel Weinberg further concluded that physical affection and warmth expressed by parents to children were predictors of a good marriage, sound mental health, and solid work success.

The love that most child psychologists recommend— even non-Christian psychologists—is unconditional love, which is loving children *no matter what.* No matter what they look like, their assets, their disabilities, or their difficult behavior. If we love our children only when they please us or meet our requirements, they grow up feeling incompetent. The more important fact to recognize, however, is that God loves us with unconditional love.

Ross Campbell, M.D., author of *How to Really Love Your Child,* speaks of a child's "emotional tank." A child does his best only if that emotional tank is kept full of love.

How do you do this?

Mostly by being available to your children and being sensitive to their needs above your own. If your children come to you needing comfort, do you reject them because you're busy, or do you stop what you are doing and hold them close for a few moments? If your children come to you with a hurt, do you tell them to get a grip, or do you listen and console?

How does this relate to Christianity? The children with parents who are always available spiritually and emotionally to them, ready to fill up their tank with love, are children whose understanding of God is that of a heavenly Father who always hears and answers prayers, and who is eager to heal, restore, mend, or reconcile.

Your children will receive your love in very practical ways:

• *Eye contact.* When you talk to your children, look into their eyes. Perhaps nothing builds them up more than engaging in frequent eye contact with you. They learn very quickly that you take them and your relationship seriously, and that you desire an intimate level of family communication with them.

• *Meaningful touching.* I'm amazed at the number of parents who touch their children only when they dress them, help them in and out of a car, or lift them up to get a drink of water. That is *not* what I mean by meaningful touch. A meaningful touch is a touch that says, "I like being with you," and "I love you." It's a touch that's meaningful to children. If they are uncomfortable with a touch, it isn't meaningful to them. Some children need lots of hugs; others like a little hug now and then but don't appreciate cuddling that distracts them from their own purposes and activities. Be sensitive to each child's needs. It's such an easy, simple thing to tousle a child's hair, touch him on the shoulder, or take her hand as you walk. Touch says to your children that you enjoy their presence and that you like to be close to them. That's a critical message to send to them.

• *Focused communication.* When your children speak, do you listen? *Really* listen? Giving your children your full attention and turning comments into conversations lets your children know that you are willing to give them the most precious commodity of time.

One of the foremost complaints of teenagers about their parents is that they cannot *talk* to their parents. It isn't that they don't want to. It's that they don't believe their parents really want to talk to them! They don't see their parents making time for conversations, being open to having conversations with them, or knowing how to converse.

Learning to talk to teenagers takes time. In fact, it takes just about the same length of time as for the children to grow from infancy to being teenagers! In other words, if you don't talk to your children while they are growing up, don't expect to be a master at communicating with them when they become teenagers.

The big issues that parents know they should discuss with children—sex, the dangers of drug use, how to handle peer pressure, and so forth—are best handled as part of an ongoing flow of conversation about these topics from the time your children are toddlers. The same holds true for your relationship with the Lord. It's a topic best interwoven into the fabric of your children's thinking from their earliest memories.

All in the Context of Love

Now, certain types of touching are inappropriate, just as stares and angry glares are inappropriate means of eye contact. Focused listening can be accusatory. All of these behaviors by themselves are neutral in and of themselves; they must be fueled by genuine godly love.

As parents, we must evaluate our hearts. Do we feel a deep genuine love for our children? Do we sense that we are loving our children to the depth that the Father would desire for us to love them?

If you feel that you are falling short, ask the Lord to give you a deeper love for your children . . . to help you relate to them with greater eye contact, touching, and listening, and to do it with love . . . to help you see your children as He sees them, objects of immense unfathomable love.

Love is also the most significant factor underlying the discipline of children. Children who know they are loved respond much more quickly to discipline than children who question a parent's love.

Keep in mind, too, that your children continue to need physical displays of love—eye contact, hugs, focused listening—all during their growing-up years and, in fact, all through life. Don't move away from your children when they hit puberty. Children still need a hug that says, "You're mine, and I'm glad about it."

Not only do children learn primarily from an emotional base in their earliest years, but they remember emotions far more than concepts. They will remember how they felt in a situation more than they will remember the details of all that happened.

Your children will remember the mood of your home, spiritually speaking—the general spiritual atmosphere, the prevailing tenor, the general feeling—more than any single moment of teaching, prayer, or Bible study.

They will remember the security they felt in established rhythms and patterns—frequent praise, regular bedtime prayer, nightly kisses and hugs before the lights went out —far more than any one prayer.

When it comes to Sunday school or church, your children will recall whether the experience was pleasant or unpleasant more so than the specifics of the lesson taught or the Scriptures read or the sermon preached.

What makes children feel good about attending church? It isn't that they feel entertained! Rather, it's being treated with kindness, respect, and loving concern. Children who feel criticized, humiliated, or second-rate at church will want to flee from the experience.

I will even go so far as to say that a lesson can be boring, but if the teacher genuinely conveys love, respect, concern, and kindness to the children in the classroom—acknowledging their spiritual potential and conveying to them the passion the teacher feels for the Lord—the children will come away with a good, positive feeling about the class.

Rather than focus on teaching principles and rules, concentrate on creating an atmosphere within your home—one of love expressed in terms of affection, communication, and respect. In so doing, you *will* be modeling the nature of God to your children.

Yet another way of modeling God's behavior to them is to . . .

Accept Your Children's Uniqueness

Recognize that your children are unique creations of God. Your spiritual gifts are not likely to be mirrored in your children. What God has called you to do in His kingdom, and the role He has given you to fulfill, may be quite different from what He has prepared for your children.

Not only should you accept the fact that your children are unique—and that no other children on the earth have ever been or will ever be given their unique talents, gifts, or personalities—but you must let them *know* that you see them as unique and that you approve of their uniqueness. Help your children explore their potential in the

Lord. Challenge them to become not all that you desire them to become but all that the Lord has designed for them to become.

Applaud your children's accomplishments. Give enthusiastic approval for their efforts. But appreciate most of all their unique humanity.

Accepting your children's uniqueness is a big part of showing unconditional love to them.

Again, that is the way our heavenly Father relates to us. He accepts each of us as His creation, a one-of-a-kind human being placed on this earth for a once-in-a-lifetime role. He stands by us as we attempt to live out His will to the best of our ability. He applauds our successes. But He loves us always for who He made us to be.

In displaying God's nature to your children, you must, of course . . .

Allow the Holy Spirit to Do His Convicting Work

If you sense that your children are being convicted by the Holy Spirit about something, allow Him to do His work. Don't step in and say, in an attempt to smooth over the struggle your children may be experiencing, "It's all right, dear," or "I'm sure it isn't all that bad," or "Don't take this so seriously." Don't attempt to diminish or dismiss the work of the Lord.

Rather, ask your children what you might do to help. Be available to discuss a situation with them. Listen closely to the real core of the issue *as your children perceive it.* Be quick to pray for your children about the matter, perhaps for them to experience forgiveness, to be healed, to have God's wisdom, or to make a deeper level of commitment to the Lord.

There's a great difference between condemnation and conviction. Condemnation is the work of human beings and of Satan. It is not an attribute of God the Father. Condemnation judges and sentences based on human or devilish criteria, with the sentence usually being one without any hope of parole, pardon, or reprieve. Condemnation puts persons down and heaps coals of guilt on their heads.

Conviction, on the other hand, is the work of the Holy Spirit. Conviction calls persons to a better choice and a better future.

Condemnation kicks persons backward. Conviction pulls persons forward.

The Spirit "Woos" Us

The Bible offers numerous examples of God seemingly intruding or intervening in the lives of His people with a dramatic display of power. The instances, however, are negative only to God's enemies. His intervention in the lives of His people is just as positive as is the negative power of His intervention in the lives of His enemies. For example, the shepherds abiding their flocks by night certainly had their slumber interrupted—but by such a glorious celestial display and by such a powerful word of hope that most of us would gladly have accepted an invitation to witness the angelic host in action.

In another example, Saul encountered a blinding light that came packaged with a divine question: "How long will you kick against Me?" Saul opted for conversion, perhaps thereby avoiding a dramatic demise. The result of such an intervention was one that brought not a shudder to the apostle Paul as he reflected on it but a great outpouring of thanksgiving for God's grace in his life.

Such moments of dramatic intervention, however, are not the norm of the Bible. They capture our attention, but they are far from the whole story. The broader picture is one of a gentle, loving Father who is ever wooing His children into a deeper and deeper relationship with Him.

One of the best studies of God's Word is an examination of the many references in which the words *tender, gentle,* and *kind* appear.

Gentleness is one attribute of the fruit of the Holy Spirit listed in Galatians 5:22–23. The apostle Paul, whom most of us don't automatically think of as being meek and mild, wrote to the Corinthians, "Now I, Paul, myself am pleading with you by the meekness and gentleness of Christ" (2 Cor. 10:1). And again to the Thessalonians he wrote, "We were gentle among you, just as a nursing mother cherishes her own children. So, affectionately longing for you, we were well pleased to impart to you not only the gospel of God, but also our own lives, because you had become dear to us" (1 Thess. 2:7–8).

To Timothy, Paul stated these words that ring with wisdom for parents as they train up children to love and serve the Lord:

> A servant of the Lord must not quarrel but be gentle to all, able to teach, patient, in humility correcting those who are in opposition, if God perhaps will grant them repentance, so that they may know the truth, and that they may come to their senses and escape the snare of the devil (2 Tim. 2:24–26).

And to Titus, Paul declared, "Remind them to be subject to rulers and authorities, to obey, to be ready for every good work, to speak evil of no one, to be peaceable, gentle, showing all humility to all men" (Titus 3:1–2).

In giving His parable of the sower and the seed falling on different types of soil, Jesus taught, "The ones [seeds] that fell on the good ground are those who, having heard the word with a noble and a good heart, keep it and bear fruit with patience" (Luke 8:15).

Luke asserted that the very presence of Jesus on the earth was "through the tender mercy of our God" (Luke 1:78).

These verses and so many others point toward God's wooing of humanity—reaching out in tenderness and nurturing love to draw humankind unto Himself.

We know in our human relationships that kindness, love, and gentleness attract, just as rudeness, hate, and roughness repel. Surely that same principle holds true as we join with the Holy Spirit in gently drawing our children closer and closer to the Lord Jesus.

In my opinion, there's something drastically wrong if a four-year-old is made to feel condemnation or guilt. However, in cases where the parent sees the child as "out"— and one who "must be brought in"—condemnation and guilt are what the child *will* feel.

Approaching a Day of
Personal Commitment

When you allow the Holy Spirit to do His convicting work in your children's lives . . .

And when you do your part in displaying God's nature as one of nurturing, affectionate, edifying love . . .

The day *will* come when children are ready to confess Jesus as their personal Savior and Lord. I believe with all my heart that such a day is marked and ordained on God's calendar for each child. That day may well come, however, sooner than later and often sooner than you expect.

That is part of God's plan. He *wants* a relationship to be established with your children directly and personally at the earliest possible time.

Don't assume from my sharing with you about household salvation that children can live under the banner of your salvation forever. Jesus Christ paid too high a price for people to live in a once-removed-relationship with the Father, and that's what your children would have if they never moved fully into a personal relationship with the Lord God once they reach the age where they comprehend the consequences of a willful decision to love and serve the Lord or *not* to love and serve the Lord.

The day comes when children must take their own stand for the Lord. Let's remind ourselves of what Paul affirmed: "If you confess with your mouth the Lord Jesus and believe in your heart that God has raised Him from the dead, you will be saved. For with the heart one believes unto righteousness, and with the mouth confession is made unto salvation" (Rom. 10:9–10).

In many ways, your children can be trained to believe with their hearts the righteous way to live. They can learn, by training and by experience, what it means to live in right relationship with the Creator. They can know the warmth of fellowship with the Lord and be comfortable in His presence.

The time comes, however, when your children must confess with their mouths that Jesus is the Savior and risen Lord. Using an earlier analogy, the day comes when your children must get off your shoes and be full partners with the Lord in a divine dance. The day comes when your children must stand before God's throne alone and declare solely by their own will that they have chosen the faith that has been chosen for them by their parents.

Again, that day can and often does come sooner than you expect it. And again, that day comes not because you push it, promote it, demand it, or require it. It comes *as* you allow the Holy Spirit to do His work and as you model the loving nature of God to your children.

God Has a Unique
Timetable for Each Child

Not only has God created each child as a unique and irreplaceable human being, but He has each child on a unique timetable for spiritual growth and development.

After one of our appearances on Trinity Broadcasting Network, on which my wife, Cynthia, and I discussed this very issue, we received more than a thousand letters relating to what we had said. We read every one, and we wept over many of them.

One letter was already tear-stained when we received it. A mother wrote, "My seven-year-old boy walked the aisle of our church when the pastor gave an invitation to receive Jesus and join the church. The person who met him at the altar turned him around physically and sent him back, saying, 'You're too young right now to be saved.' "

Friend, doesn't that break your heart?

The child was experiencing a work of the Holy Spirit, tugging at his heart to make a life-changing, future-altering decision. And then he came face-to-face with an adult who immediately, without spiritual discernment about what was happening in the young child's life, denied him access to full status within the body of Christ.

What about a church that says, "You may become a full member when you are twelve but not before"? Such a church has taken over the work of the Holy Spirit and has said, in effect, "We can't trust the Holy Spirit to work in the lives of our children or to bring them to a full acceptance of and confession of Jesus as Lord. Instead, we will decide on the basis of recitation and understanding of head knowledge *about* God whether a child shall be made a full member of our community of faith."

The Holy Spirit has a timetable for every child in your church to come to a fullness of understanding about who the Lord God is and what God requires of us as human beings—acceptance of Jesus as our sacrifice for sin, and a desire to love and serve Him as His representatives on the earth. Some children may come to that awareness and be ready to make that decision at age five! Others at age ten! Others at fourteen! Others at still other ages. It is not our human prerogative to decide arbitrarily that children are old enough or too young.

How old do children need to be before they can make a sound, lasting decision to love and serve Jesus as Savior and Lord? As old as their ability to perceive that is what they want to do.

Helping Your Children
Take That Final Step

How can you tell when your children are ready to take the last step toward making a personal confession that Jesus Christ is Savior and Lord?

They will probably show some signs of spiritual unrest. They may ask "how" and "why" and "what if" questions. You might ask them at such times, "Are you wondering if everything is okay between you and God?"

Other children sometimes feel a greater desire to hear about heaven or hell. The question you ask your children might be, "Are you wondering about where you will spend eternity?"

If they answer yes to either question, even with the veiled yes answer of "well, sorta," you can respond, "There's a way to be free of these doubts and settle this issue once and for all." Lead your children in a sinner's prayer and point out several verses to assure them of their salvation.

Parents should know how to lead their children in a prayer of repentance and forgiveness. Here's a simple prayer for you to study and even memorize. Ask your children to repeat the prayer after you, phrase by phrase:

Heavenly Father, I want to know with certainty that I am in right relationship with You. I know I have done things that have disappointed You or have hurt You. I am truly sorry for those things. I want to live my life in a way that is according to Your plan for me. Please forgive me of my sins. Please fill me with Your Holy Spirit and help me to live the rest of my life in a way that is pleasing to You. I believe in what Jesus Christ did on the cross for me. I accept Him as the sacrifice for my sins, and I confess right now that He is my Savior and my Lord. I believe that You are forgiving me of my sins and that I will live with You forever in heaven. I accept Your gift of a new life beginning right now. I pray all of this in Jesus' name. Amen.

(Explain to your children that *amen* means "let it be so" or "so be it.")

Read with your children these verses of Scripture that confirm the importance and surety of what they have just prayed:

• "For God so loved the world that He gave His only begotten Son, that whoever believes in Him should not perish but have everlasting life" (John 3:16).

• "If you confess with your mouth the Lord Jesus and believe in your heart that God has raised Him from the dead, you will be saved. For with the heart one believes unto righteousness, and with the mouth confession is made unto salvation" (Rom. 10:9–10).

• "If we confess our sins, He is faithful and just to forgive us our sins and to cleanse us from all unrighteousness" (1 John 1:9).

Assure your children that no outside force can ever take away from them what they have experienced, remove from them the Word of God that they have hidden in their hearts, or cause the Holy Spirit of God to depart from them.

What If You Don't Know Whether Your Children Have Made a Confession of Faith?

Many parents have said to me, "I don't know for sure if my children have made a personal confession of faith. I think they have, but I just don't know."

There's only one way to find out. Ask.

Don't be embarrassed. Don't be shy about it. You are dealing with the eternal fate of your children. Ask simply and directly, "Have you ever made a personal confession of your faith in Jesus Christ? Have you ever received Him into your life as your personal Savior? Have you made Him the Lord of your life?"

If they have, they will have an opportunity to share a positive word of witness with you.

If your children have not, the question raises in their minds the fact that this is an important issue to you, and that it is one about which they must make a decision.

Don't press your children for a decision. Simply ask the question.

If your children answer, "No, I haven't," you might ask, "Would you like to? Wouldn't you like to settle that issue once and for all?"

If they say they aren't ready to make that commitment, don't press the point. Again, allow the Holy Spirit to use your comments to do *His* work. You can, however, assure your children that you will continue to intercede for them, and that you look forward to the day when they are spiritually mature enough to take that step.

This discussion is vital for you to have with teenagers before they leave your home to begin college or to enter the work force.

As a parent, you need to know where your children stand with the Lord. In hearing their answers, you gain insight into how to continue praying for your children.

Bringing this issue to the forefront of teenagers' thinking is not counter to the nature of God. The Lord throughout the Bible deals with people in a very direct, honest way. In wooing and convicting, He isn't underhanded. He doesn't sneak up on your children. His compelling love is open, transparent, and guileless.

The greatest act of compassion you can ever show to your children is to express concern about their eternal souls. And again, that concern is to be shared in love, not with a spirit of condemnation.

6

Training Up Your Children Through Simulations

The righteous man walks in his integrity;
His children are blessed after him.
                    —Proverbs 20:7

We as Christian parents are not commanded by the Lord to raise children. Peas, carrots, and corn are raised. Raising involves providing only those things necessary for growth.

We, on the other hand, are required by the Lord to *train* our children. Training involves providing the necessary things for growth and then guiding that growth.

In fact, the formal definition of *to train* includes these phrases: "to mold the character; to make obedient to orders; to prepare for a contest; to point in an exact direction." When you train your children, you do all four of these things:

• helping to mold their character into the image and likeness of Jesus Christ.

• seeking to develop obedience as a character trait in them so that they might always be obedient to the Lord.

• preparing them for spiritual contests with the enemy of their souls.

• pointing them in the direction of heaven.

Let's recognize, too, that . . .

In training up our children to love and serve the Lord, we are also training up, to a certain degree, their children and their children's children.

Those who study intergenerational behavior patterns tell us with increasing confidence that most of what we do as parents is a mirror image of what our parents modeled for us when we were children.

A godly parent raises a godly child to *be* a godly parent.

The decisions you make about raising your children today will affect your family for many decades to come!

"To Train" Is a Command

The Lord has commanded us to train our children. It's not an option. It's not a request. It's a requirement.

The command of God to train children is no more explicitly stated than in Deuteronomy 4:9–10:

> Only take heed to yourself, and diligently keep yourself, lest you forget the things your eyes have seen, and lest they depart from your heart all the days of your life. And teach them to your children and your grandchildren, especially concerning the day you stood before the LORD your God in Horeb, when the LORD said to me, "Gather the people to Me, and I will let them hear My words, that they may learn to fear Me all the days they live on the earth, and that they may teach their children."

Spiritual education of children was not considered to be either automatic or optional. The spiritual training of children requires intention, attention, and diligence.

The good news is that the Lord provides a way for us to train our children.

Training with a Goal

Proverbs 22:6 is one of the most famous verses in the Bible:

Train up a child in the way he should go,
And when he is old he will not depart from it.

I'd like to point out three things about that verse.

First, notice that there is a way a child *should* go. The Bible does not at any time advocate that a parent should give a child free rein to do, say, or believe whatever he wants.

The way a child *should* go is what the Bible is all about. The Bible is the ultimate handbook for Christian behavior; it is the owner's manual for effective Christlike living on this earth.

This verse is a great challenge to us as parents to teach our children the deep truths of the Bible, a matter we will discuss further in the next two chapters.

Second, notice that this verse presents a biblical maxim. If we will do our part in training up a child in the way he should go, we are establishing the greatest possible likelihood that he *will not depart from it* when he is old.

A mother once said to me, "I had hoped that 'when he is old' meant age twelve. I came to realize that in the case of our daughter, that verse meant when she reached age twenty-four and had a child of her own."

This verse does not promise that a child may not rebel. It does promise that a child can never get away from the influence of a godly foundation, and that in time and in God's grace, the child will return to the way in which he has been led.

Third, notice that this verse uses the word *train*. It is the

99

same word used for military behavior. Indeed, training is the process used any time a teacher desires that a student make decisions on an instinctual, spontaneous, habitual basis.

A fighter pilot has no time to think through what actions he should take once an enemy plane fires on him. His response must be lightning quick, as an instinct, if he is to survive combat. How does that fighter pilot acquire such instincts? He certainly isn't born with them, although part of his physical attributes may be quick reflexes. No, the instincts are acquired through *training*. And that training has four key components: simulation, repetition, discipline, and real-time practice.

The fighter pilot entering combat has had literally thousands of hours of simulation—using real-to-life instrument panels, videos, and signals. He has gone through the exercises critical to skillful flying so many times that he feels almost as if he could fly in his sleep. He has become disciplined in body and mind, and he has been soundly reprimanded for mistakes that might lead to peril. And he's been up in the air. He's logged countless hours of airtime in a wide variety of weather conditions and through numerous war game exercises.

He is as prepared as he can be for the moment when real rockets begin to fly his way.

This same principle of training is what Christian adult behavior should be all about. We should not have to think about or ponder what to do when faced with a temptation or crisis. Our spiritual instincts should already be developed from childhood. We should know immediately how to respond—with faith. How to pray. What to say. How to use the Word of God as a sword of the Spirit. What to believe for. How to help others.

We should have been through countless hours of simulation, repeated drills, and practice sessions. Our habits of Christlike behavior should not only be second nature to us. They should *be* our nature. We should have a thoroughly developed Christian mind-set toward life—a characteristic that the Scriptures call having "the mind of Christ."

Developing this mind of Christ in our children should be our ultimate desire for all that we do to prepare and educate our children to follow Jesus Christ. It is the goal of our spiritual training process in our children's lives. In terms that educators use when they develop curriculum and lesson plans, "the mind of Christ" is our educational objective, which will manifest itself in a wide variety of behaviors considered to be Christlike.

Ultimately, our goal is to so train our children that they will respond as if by instinct, habit, or intuition to a situation in the same way that Jesus Christ Himself would respond should He face the same situation on this earth.

Your Spiritual Life Is Your Children's Best Simulation Experience

Simulation experiences are critical to learning. A simulation is a situation that is set up to be so much like the real thing that you can hardly tell it isn't real. In many ways, your including your children in your spiritual reality is like a highly sophisticated simulation exercise for them.

As you pray and include your children in that activity, they learn to pray. They mimic your words. They mirror your concerns. They may even take on your tone of voice. Such prayer does not originally spring forth from the lips, or hearts, of your children. It is a learned behavior. Your children copy the behavior they see before them. The day will come, however, when your children no longer need to copy but will respond to the Lord in prayer using their own words. They will pray about their own concerns, using language and a tone of voice that are uniquely theirs. In this way, a simulation prepares for and leads to the real thing.

A key principle, therefore, in training up your children is this:

Allow your children to do for themselves what *you* consider to be the most important aspects of your relationship with the Lord. The foremost hallmarks of a Christian's relationship with the Lord may well be . . .

1. The Process of Confession, Repentance, and Forgiveness

Nearly every adult Christian I've ever met has affirmed to me the importance of ongoing confession, repentance, and forgiveness in life. See their importance for your children, too!

Children need to know that it's possible to live without guilt.

Stop to consider that statement for a few moments. As parents, we generally consider one of our prime responsibilities to be that of teaching our children the difference between right and wrong, between acceptable behavior and unacceptable behavior. Listen to the average parent of an average two-year-old and you might think that both have a vocabulary of one word: *Don't.*

"Don't do that"; "Don't say that"; "Don't go there"; "Don't touch that"; "Don't climb on that"; "Just don't."

At the same time, of course, the parent is teaching positives: "Say, 'Please' "; "Say, 'Thank you' "; "Use your fork"; "Brush your teeth"; "Here's how you tie your shoes"; "Give Grandma a hug"; "Share your toys."

Good and bad behavior.

The day quickly comes when children know that they have done something wrong and the result in the human psyche is to expect punishment. Furthermore, children come to expect that the punishment will completely purge the wrong committed and the behavior slate will be wiped clean—which is another way of saying forgiveness. When punishment and forgiveness do not follow inappropriate behavior, children get a mixed signal. They conclude either that the behavior was *not* wrong or that justice hasn't been carried out. The conclusion that the behavior was not wrong, of course, can be disastrous. That unmitigated conclusion is probably at the root of most juvenile delinquency. Thousands of children in our nation today conclude that there's nothing wrong about a certain behavior. They simply haven't been taught right from wrong.

Christian parents rarely allow that conclusion to stand. They are usually quick to help children learn "do and don't behavior." The error is more likely that wrong behavior is not confessed and absolved. What happens? The resulting feeling that justice has not been carried out quickly becomes a load of *guilt.*

Guilt is a terrible burden to human beings, whether eighty years old or eight years old. Feeling guilt means knowing we have done something that has violated the code of right and wrong.

Guilt is something we can't erase on our own. The only way to eliminate guilt is through forgiveness from someone greater than ourselves. Ignoring wrong behavior doesn't absolve guilt. It only buries further the sense of guilt.

What must a parent do? Give your children an opportunity to confess wrongdoings, to repent of them, and to experience forgiveness.

That can happen easily and naturally if you develop in your family a habit of bedtime prayer, including a prayer for forgiveness as part of that prayer. You may want to ask your children, "Is there anything that you know you've done today for which you'd like God to forgive you?" And then lead them in a prayer of forgiveness or allow them to pray spontaneously their own prayer. Children can begin to pray this way on their own from the age of about three.

The threefold confess-repent-forgiveness process can

be stated in these simple prayer terms that even young children understand:

• "I admit it." Encourage children to own up to their sins and to take responsibility for them. Don't dismiss wrong behavior lightly with a "that's okay" pat on the psyche. Children know more than we parents sometimes recognize that it isn't okay. Give your children the freedom to say, "I did it or said it or felt it. I admit it."

• "I'm sorry. I don't want to do this again." Repentance includes both honest heartfelt remorse and a desire not to repeat the offense. Help your children learn both aspects of repentance. It isn't enough just to say, "I'm sorry"— which sometimes can be interpreted, "I'm sorry I got caught," or "I'm sorry I have to admit this." Children must also see that true sorrow for a behavior includes a desire not to repeat it.

• "Please forgive me." This prayer statement must be voiced with faith that God indeed will be true to His promise to forgive. One of the best Bible memory verses you can teach children is 1 John 1:9: "If we confess our sins, He is faithful and just to forgive us our sins and to cleanse us from all unrighteousness." Explain to young children that this means, in a nutshell, "When we ask God to forgive us, He always does." Not sometimes, but every time. Not just for some sins, but for all sins. Not just for a few people, but for every person who asks His forgiveness.

In training your children to seek God's forgiveness, you will also want to model forgiving behavior for your children. Be quick to forgive them when they come to you and say, "I did something wrong. I'm sorry. Please forgive me."

That is not to say that some form of punishment or retribution may not be required to reinforce their repentance, that is, their desire never to repeat the behavior. Even so, any form of punishment should be followed with hugs of forgiveness so that your children are completely assured that the bad behavior record has been cleared and they stand in good relationship with you.

Furthermore, in modeling this process for your children, let them hear you confess your faults in prayer. Don't let them grow up thinking that you are perfect. That's a terrible impression for children to have—it so often results in a spirit of striving for perfection that can never be fully achieved. You can say, "I'm sorry, Lord, that I lost my patience while driving on the freeway today. Please help me to see those who cut me off on the road as You see them, with compassion. Help me to relax and enjoy my time in the car by talking to You. Please forgive me." Or you can pray, "Father, I'm sorry I was so irritable today with Sally and Jimmy. I need You to help me to be more patient and kind and not to feel so stressed out. Please forgive me and help me to have more of Your joy tomorrow."

You may say, "Well, won't my children lose respect for me if I pray this way in front of them?" No, they'll have more respect for you in the long run of their lives. They might lose respect if they see you not making an attempt to change the things you have prayed about or if they feel your prayer is insincere. To that end, you must pray with the same attitude that you encourage in your children: an honest, straightforward, sincere communication with the heavenly Father. No con jobs. No halfhearted words. Let your children see you model sincere, genuine confession and repentance. They'll come away with a much more honest appraisal of God's forgiveness!

In this area of confession, repentance, and forgiveness, make certain that your children understand the difference between a mistake and a sin.

Mistakes are errors that do not involve the will. Sin always involves the will.

Tripping and falling and ripping one's dress is a mistake, not a sin. Knocking over one's glass of milk while gesturing in a conversation is a mistake, not a sin.

On the other hand, saying rude things to an adult involves the will. So does disobeying a rule not to enter the neighbor's garden and trample on the flowers.

We adults generally use the phrase, "I'm sorry," in dealing with both mistakes and sins. Indeed, we can feel sorrow about mistakes, and it's right to apologize for them. Recognize, however, that your children hear "I'm sorry" only in relationship to mess-ups. They need to learn to identify the difference between a clumsy, accidental mistake and a willful act.

True repentance involves the will, and that's why we include in our "I'm sorry" prayer the statement, "I don't want to do this again."

I find it helpful to conclude a forgiveness prayer with one final element.

• "Please help me, God, not to do this again." This part of prayer helps children immensely. It puts God on their side as an ally in the process of living, not a fierce judge waiting to pounce on unconfessed behavior. Encourage your children to pray this prayer when they feel tempted to repeat a wrong behavior, "Please help me, God, not to give in to this temptation."

Finally, explain to your children the difference between temptation and sin. Temptation is a desire to sin that the enemy plants in our minds. Temptation is a "want to" attitude toward something that we have been taught is wrong. It is not a sin unless we follow through and do the deed. Even young children can understand this point.

They know it's wrong to hit a brother or sister. Nevertheless, they *want* to do so at times. That's a temptation. It isn't a sin, however, unless they haul off and slug their sibling. The learned prayer, "Help me, God, not to do this," is the best prayer to ward off temptation. It causes children to stop and think and, in so doing, to develop responsible responses to life.

2. Thanksgiving, Praise, and Worship

These aspects of Christian life are just as vital as confession-repentance-forgiveness to most adults. Thanksgiving, praise, and worship build a relationship with a loving Father.

Let your children hear you praise God

• often. Don't be stingy with your praise and thanksgiving.

• in short bursts of ongoing response to life: "Oh, praise God! Isn't this wonderful news!"

• as a part of bedtime prayer: "We are so thankful tonight, Lord, for all that You have done for us today, for all that You are, for all that You will do and be for us tomorrow."

Encourage your children's praises. You may want to begin a prayer session with them by holding them close and saying, "What shall we thank God for?"

Don't be surprised at some things your children say in a thanksgiving prayer: "Winning the game" . . . "passing the test" . . . "remembering to go to the bathroom during recess" . . . "ice cream for dessert" . . . "Making the stars."

Nothing is too grand or too trivial for thanksgiving. No sincere expression of praise or thanksgiving should be negated or considered to be inappropriate unless it is voiced with sarcasm.

Rather than be concerned that your children's praises and thanksgivings might not be lofty enough, rejoice that they feel free to express what they like and appreciate. That's a behavior worth carrying into adulthood.

Teach your children some of the names and attributes of the Father and Son and Holy Spirit and incorporate them into your prayer life.

Your children can learn at a very early age that God is Jehovah Jireh, our provider. (In fact, children at the age of about four have a capacity to learn and remember some of these Hebrew phrases even better than their parents can learn and remember them!) Children delight in thanking and praising God for being Jehovah Nissi, our banner; El Shaddai, the God of Strength; or the Lord God almighty, the One with all might.

Perhaps the greatest name of God that we can teach our children is the one that Jesus Himself taught us, Abba, Father. Even children with less-than-perfect earthly fathers (which includes all of us) can understand the concept of a Father who never leaves us, never disappoints us, is always ready and willing to hear us (at any time of night or day), and is on our side forever, desiring only our best. Talk to your children about their heavenly Father or our Father in heaven. They'll get the picture!

The names and attributes of Jesus are equally appealing to children. I overheard a five-year-old girl praying one time, "Jesus, thank You for being the Rose of Sharon." She may not have known the full implications of "Sharon" or "rose," but she did know that the phrase "Rose of Sharon" evoked a sense of beauty and awe in her. She loved the sound of those words, and she loved the idea that Jesus could be as lovely as a rose. I find sound theology in that!

Children have great meaning for these names:

• Savior—the One who saves us from the devil.
• Teacher—the One who shows us the best way to live.
• Lord—the One we live for.
• Eternal King—The one who sits on heaven's throne forever.
• Friend of friends—the best friend your children will ever have.

The Holy Spirit is easily understood by children as our Helper—the One who helps us to withstand temptations and to make right choices. He is the Spirit of truth—the One who will bring to light the truth of any situation. He is the still small voice of God that speaks in our spirits and lets us know if we are doing something right or wrong. He is our strength—the One who helps us to follow through on convictions and do God's will on the earth.

Give your children a full picture of God. Don't limit their divine imagination about God.

I am amazed at times to hear adults tell me that as children, they thought God was mean—a stern old judge with a long white beard, quick to send sinners to hell—Jesus was a nice man who healed people, and the Holy Spirit was rather ephemeral, a true ghost of almost the Casper variety.

Don't leave your children with those impressions. Give them the full scoop on the Trinity. The more attributes of God the Father, Son, and Holy Spirit you can pull out of Bible stories, the more names for Father, Son, and Holy Spirit you can teach your children, the more they will comprehend the full majesty of God and the depth and breadth and height of His love for us, His children.

Sprinkle all of your daily activities with thanksgiving and praise. Make praise a spontaneous part of your life, and give voice to it frequently. Don't wait until church time to proclaim God's goodness in a way that your children can hear and understand it.

Are you witnessing a magnificent sunset with your children? "Praise God. Just look at the sunset He is creating for our pleasure! Praise God that He created us, too."

Are you enjoying a particularly well-cooked meal? "Praise God for giving us the ability to provide and cook this food. He truly is Jehovah Jireh, isn't He?"

Have you come home from a tough day at work, grateful to be at home where you can relax with those you love? "Praise God, I'm home. The Lord really gave me extra strength today, and I sure am glad He gave you to me as a family that I can come home to."

Has a child brought home a good grade on a report?

"Praise God for this good report. We know that all good things come from You, God, and I thank You that You gave Josh the discipline to research this report and the ability to write it so well."

Such praise and thanksgiving prayers may sound artificial to you the first few times you give voice to them. As with so many things, praise and thanksgiving demand practice. The more you offer praise and thanksgiving to the Lord, the more natural they will seem to you. In many ways, you are building a habit for yourself and for your children—a habit to respond to the good things of life, and to see all good things as coming from the Father. Teach your children these words of Jesus: "I have come that they may have life, and that they may have it more abundantly" (John 10:10).

Point out examples of an abundant life to your children. Call their attention to the fact that God's great gifts of peace, love, and joy are a part of what God has given to us and for which we can be thankful. God's gift to us is our family, our house, our neighborhood, our city. He provides daily for our needs—what we eat, what we wear, a safe bed to sleep in, all that we have and consider important for life.

Give your children the confidence that beyond you, God is concerned about their welfare. He desires only the best for your children and acts on their behalf.

3. Prayer and the Exercise of Faith

Prayer is petitioning God. In terms children understand, it is asking for something.

Give your children an opportunity to ask God for the things they both need and want.

• "Please keep me safe tonight as I sleep. Don't let me have any bad dreams."

• "Please help me find the library book I have lost."

- "Please help me get along with my teacher tomorrow."
- "Please keep us from getting sick."
- "Please give me a bicycle."

Such prayer develops a wonderful habit in children's lives of looking to God, their heavenly Father, for what they desire.

You as a parent meet many of your children's needs. That's your role in their lives. But God has not asked you to meet all their wants. Neither has He asked you to take His place as the supplier of their lives. Give them an opportunity to trust God on their own.

Actually, the parent who hears a prayerful request, "Please give me a bicycle, God," and then turns around and buys that child a bicycle may circumvent God's will. The Lord may have an entirely unique and wonderful way of providing an answer to the prayer that doesn't remotely involve you. In providing the bicycle, you may be robbing your child of a true faith-building adventure.

In asking God for specific things in life, of course, your children take a risk with their faith. They put their faith on the line to believe for something. Your concern as a parent naturally leads you to ask, "But what if God doesn't hear that prayer or doesn't choose to answer it?"

The reality is that God *always* hears and *always* answers. Assure your children of that fact. God always hears their prayers, and God always answers them. Children don't have to wait until they are fully grown for God to hear and answer. They don't have to be perfect for God to hear and answer. God hears and answers because He loves us and desires to be in communication with us and to bless us.

At the same time, explain to your children that God as the heavenly Father answers prayers in the same ways that you as a parent sometimes answer your children.

• "No." Your children never like to hear no, but they usually understand a "no" with a reason. The main reason for a parent to tell children they can't have something or do something is for the protection of the children (physically, emotionally, or spiritually) or for the higher good of the whole family. As a parent, you are able to see something or know something that your children don't know about a situation. (Sometimes that "something" is only a hunch, but as a parent, sometimes a hunch is all you have to go on.)

Our heavenly Father answers us in the same way. He sees things from a higher perspective than we see things. A good verse to back this up is Isaiah 55:9: "For as the heavens are higher than the earth, so are My ways higher than your ways, and My thoughts than your thoughts."

Our heavenly Father doesn't tell us no to be mean to us; He is doing something for our protection—even though we may not fully understand that—or for the good of His entire family, all of the Christians everywhere around the world.

• "Not now." Your children have probably heard you give this answer more times than they can count! "Someday you can spend the night with a friend" . . . "someday you can stay up later" . . . "someday you can go by yourself."

Our heavenly Father also has a timing for our lives. Some things require us to grow up a little in our faith. In other instances, we may need to make some adjustments in our lives before we can be in the best position to receive what we are asking of God. For example, asking God for a puppy may not be a request God can answer as long as the family lives in an apartment building that doesn't allow pets. It may be a request God can answer when the family moves to a single-family dwelling or a new apartment.

• "Yes, but." Sometimes God will ask us to modify our request.

In parent-child terms, you might have determined that a certain toy is not suitable for your children. That doesn't mean you don't want your children to have *any* toys. A toy of a different type may be just fine!

The same holds true for the way our heavenly Father answers children's prayer requests. Sometimes it's okay for your children to have something in general terms but not in the specifics they pray. Point out to them that God isn't saying no. He's saying, "Yes, but here's something that is even better than what you requested."

• "Yes." This is the answer, of course, that we all want when we pray. To get this answer, however, we must ask in the will of heaven. That's the qualifier the Lord put on our prayers when He taught us to pray, "Your kingdom come. Your will be done on earth as it is in heaven" (Luke 11:2).

How can we know if we are praying in heaven's will? It is heaven's will if it's something that will further the presence of God on this earth and be a witness for Him.

In terms your children can readily understand, you might explain heaven's will in this way: "Is it something that will help people love God more? Is it something that will bring joy to God's heart? Is it something that will make all of the angels of heaven happy?"

Enjoying a safe night's sleep, finding a library book, getting along with a teacher, having good health—and even receiving a new bicycle—can all qualify!

If your children are disappointed that God hasn't answered their prayers in just the way they desire, encourage them to pray, "Father, You must have a reason. I don't understand it. I trust You anyway to do what is right for me."

Such a prayer calls children's attention away from perceived loss or disappointment and puts it back on a loving and generous God who always has their best interests at the center of His heart.

Are any prayer requests too big?   A parent once asked me, "Is there anything too big for my child to ask for?"

I said, "Such as?"

She said, "Well, I heard my child praying that her grandmother will be healed of cancer. I'm afraid that my child will think God doesn't love her or isn't a good God if my mother-in-law dies and her prayer isn't answered."

I said, "Does your child believe God *can* heal her grandmother?"

"Yes."

"Does your child believe God *wants* to heal her grandmother?"

"Oh, yes."

"Do *you* believe God can and wants to heal your mother-in-law?"

"Well, I'm not sure," the woman responded honestly.

I said, "Let your child pray. She has faith to believe for healing—faith that you don't have. We don't know how God will answer. We do know that He asks us to pray *with faith believing.*"

Always be honest with your children about prayer. As long as we are on this earth, we cannot and will not ever fully understand the importance of prayer. There's a mystery about prayer that cannot be penetrated. We can know this: Prayer is God's idea. He has asked us to voice our needs to Him in prayer and to intercede in prayer for others. He has invited us to be a part of His process of working on this earth.

It's up to us to pray. It's up to God to answer our prayers as He desires.

We have no real excuse for *not* praying, not even if we are disappointed in God's answers.

Finally, let your children hear you pray for them. Let

them hear your heart's desire for them, both in the present and in the future.

That is not, of course, to be taken as an opportunity to superimpose your will on your children. It is an opportunity to petition the Father for your children's

- health.
- safety—at play, at school, at night.
- ability to play peacefully and cooperatively with other children.
- deliverance from evil.
- ability to do their best at whatever they attempt.
- ability to respect and honor their elders, including grandparents, other older relatives, teachers, ministers, Sunday school teachers, baby-sitters, and all others who may be given authority over them.
- spiritual growth and development—including the day you anticipate your children making their own confession of the Lord Jesus as Lord.
- manifestation of Spirit fruit—love, joy, peace, long-suffering, kindness, goodness, faithfulness, gentleness, and self-control. (See Gal. 5:22–23; this list of spiritual attributes, by the way, is an excellent list to post in your home—perhaps in calligraphy or needlework—as a constant reminder to all in your family of the traits you are desiring to exhibit to one another.)
- freedom from anything and anyone who would try to influence them in ways that are harmful physically, emotionally, mentally, or spiritually.
- ability to keep God's commandments.
- sensitivity toward the things of the Lord and a discernment of what is good and evil in the Lord's eyes.
- hearts, that they might always be tender, and that they might always have a deep desire to love the Lord and to serve others.
- awareness and development of unique gifts, talents, and God-given traits.

- coming to know the will of God for their lives and responding with a heartfelt desire to fulfill it.
- future as law-abiding citizens.
- future as fully active, faithful, contributing church members.
- spirit to always remain sensitive to the convicting power of the Holy Spirit.
- future as mighty spiritual warriors and soul winners.
- ultimate future home with you, the Lord Jesus, and all other Christians in heaven for all eternity.

And there's so much more!

You'll note that this list focuses on traits you desire to see developed in your children. It is not a list of achievements. It is not a prescription for their future careers. It is *not* a list that builds in dependency upon you as a parent. I once heard a mother pray for her son, "Lord, let him always have a desire to live here with us in peace." I felt certain that she was praying that her son would never run away in rebellion. Her prayer, however, might have been construed by her son to be an invitation to live in the family home forever as a dependent child.

Here is a simple rule about prayer: Pray for your children as you believe the Lord Jesus is praying for them. The Scriptures tell us that Jesus Christ sits at the right hand of the Father making constant intercession for us. (See Rom. 8:34.) What do you believe Jesus is praying for you and your children? Surely, it is that your children might have a personal relationship with Him forevermore and grow up into the fullness of His likeness on this earth.

When you pray with your children, especially with preschoolers, be sure to pray in very concrete terms. Pray that her skinned knee will heal, his cut finger will stop bleeding, the dog next door will never bite her, and he will learn to ride his bicycle without needing the training wheels.

Encourage your children to look for signs of God's answers and, when they see them, to give praise and thanksgiving for them.

4. Giving

A fourth hallmark of Christian living deemed to be highly important for adults is giving. The same can hold for children and is perhaps the most frequently overlooked sign of Christian living in the lives of children.

Why don't we expect our children to give? I believe it is owing, in part, to a belief that our children don't have anything to give. Such a belief vastly underestimates the capability of God-fearing children in a Christian home to give and to give spontaneously.

The gift might be a hug, a kiss, a tender touch.

It might be a picture created with crayons or paint.

It might be a childmade greeting card.

It might be a stone or shell or bouquet of autumn leaves.

It might be a personal story, written and illustrated.

It might be a "gift certificate" for doing an extra chore around the house.

It might be a batch of chocolate chip cookies baked for and delivered to a family experiencing a crisis.

Encourage your children to become givers—and to give with joy.

Teach your children how to give a word of hope or encouragement to others who seem down, hurt, or scared. I once overheard a four-year-old say to her two-year-old brother who was about to go into a Sunday school class by himself for the first time, "I know you're scared to do this. I was, too. But I know you can do it, and I know Jesus is going to help you." That's a good word at any age!

When the time comes for the offering plate to be passed in church, make sure that young children have something to give. It might be only a nickel or dime. Don't let the plate pass by without your children having the satisfaction of putting in something as a gift. You'll be building a lifelong habit of supporting God's work.

When your children get to the age of receiving a regular allowance, insist that they give a portion of that to the work of the Lord. Require it. (After all, our heavenly Father requires it of us.) Children need to learn how to earn money and how to tithe and save out of that money.

Talk about what the gifts help to do—and again, be concrete in your examples:

- The care and upkeep of your church
- Choir robes and music for the choir
- The care of your pastors and their families
- Sunday school materials
- Help for missionaries and evangelists to take the gospel to those who have never heard it
- Bibles and other literature for missionaries to use when they talk to people who speak languages different from your own
- Outreach programs of your church, such as feeding, clothing, and housing homeless families
- Church youth activities
- Gasoline for the church bus

Dealing with giving in concrete terms helps your children learn about some functions of the church—especially things that require money—and also lets them feel that they have a vital part in keeping the lights on and the church doors open.

Point out to your children that all gifts are important to the Lord, regardless of their size, because the Lord looks upon the heart to see how and why the gift is being made. The story of the widow who gave two mites is a good one to share with children. They can relate to the fact that they don't have much money, either!

Show your paycheck to your children. Sit down with

them and say, "This is how much we made, and we are tithing this much to God's work." Let them see you write out the check and watch you put it into the offering plate the next Sunday. You can make no more powerful statement about giving.

Children's values about money will be in direct relationship to what they give. I believe that with all my heart. A child who is allowed to purchase a sixty-dollar pair of jeans in the mall on Saturday and then is handed a dollar bill to put into the offering plate the next day is not going to have a high regard for the church.

Stewardship is a topic closely aligned with giving. Talk to your children in terms of our responsibility as human beings to give all of our lives to the Lord. Truly, all of our time, talents, achievements, and resources come from His hand and are worthy to be given back to Him.

Stewardship of time and available natural resources is a part of God's command to us in Genesis to take care of the earth. Every child can grasp this concept. As you recycle various household items, talk to your children in terms of stewardship of our earth. Plant a tree or perhaps a vegetable or flower garden with them. Pick up litter as you go for walks together in your neighborhood. Take time to enjoy scenes of natural beauty with your children and discuss what it takes to keep an area beautiful. When you fill up your car with gasoline, point out that unleaded gasoline keeps the air cleaner than the "old style of gas" that fueled cars when you were a child. Encourage your children to see this earth as belonging to the Lord—including all of its natural wealth. He has entrusted us to take care of His earth, and we can shoulder our responsibility in many small but meaningful ways.

What does stewardship of the earth have to do with children's spiritual development? Not only is it an area of commandment by God, it is also instilling in your children your hope that their future will be wonderful. It is an expression of your faith that life will go on, and that your children's children will live in a better world than you have lived in. Hope gives children something to believe for, work for, aim at. It drives faith. As the writer to the Hebrews said, "Faith is the substance of things hoped for" (Heb. 11:1).

Point out ways in which your children can make a gift of time. You and your older children may want to volunteer together in an activity that serves your church or local community—perhaps a cleanup day at church. Do it as unto the Lord—as if it is a gift you are making to the Lord Jesus and toward the furtherance of His kingdom on the earth. Children can rake leaves or hoe weeds in the garden of a sick or elderly neighbor . . . or walk a dog for a friend who has broken an ankle . . . or run an errand for a neighbor with a newborn baby.

At Christmas time, suggest to your children that they give gifts to needy children in your church or city. Numerous opportunities are available each year for families to "adopt" a poor child or family and to give a gift that will make Christmas special. That is a wonderful opportunity for your children to learn to give sacrificially. I recently heard of parents who let each of their children make a "wish list" of four gifts. Then they buy one of the gifts for a needy child. The giving of something your children would like to have is a wonderful act of unselfishness and allows them to invest more of their emotional and spiritual selves into the gift.

Teach your children what makes a gift appropriate or inappropriate. Talk about "what if" situations as you plan special gifts or activities. A stuffed toy may not be a great gift for Grandpa, but a packet of ice-cream-counter gift certificates may please him greatly. You instill in your children a recognition that for a gift to be truly meaningful, one must first consider the recipient of the gift. What does the person need, or what would the person like? What would help most? What would help the person love the Lord more or to know more about Him?

Teach your children, also, about the gift of prayer. Intercession is a prayer gift—the giving of time and spiritual attention to another person. Children can always give the gift of a prayer to another person.

In helping your children develop a habit of giving, you may be surprised at the innovative methods of giving that they come up with on their own. Encourage spontaneous acts of giving. Applaud them. And always thank your children for gifts they give you personally or on your behalf. In that, your children will come to know the true joy of gift giving.

Simulation or the Real Thing?

Although I've referred to the spiritual activities in this chapter as simulations, they are actually the real things.

It's a little like questioning whether baby food is *real* food.

Have you ever watched a good mother feeding her young child? In go the strained peas. In go the mashed bananas. In go the pureed meats. In go the bottle of milk and the bottle of juice. The good mother is intent on feeding her child what will build her child up and cause her child to be healthier. At the same time, the good mother is creating an awareness of, a taste for, and ultimately a desire for these foods. The young child becomes so familiar with these tastes that they seem entirely normal and natural to her. Later in life, unless the child is told otherwise by peers or the good foods are so poorly prepared that they no longer taste like what she knew as an infant, the child will continue to like the same vegetables and fruits as a preschooler, as a teenager, as an adult.

HELPING YOUR CHILDREN WALK WITH GOD

The principle of good spiritual nourishment operates the same way.

Give your children an opportunity to repent and to receive the freeing feeling of forgiveness . . .

Give your children an opportunity to offer thanksgiving and praise . . .

Give your children an opportunity to pray and to believe God for the things that they need and desire . . .

Give your children a taste of the Lord's power flowing through their bodies to make them whole . . .

Give your children an opportunity to experience the presence of God through communicating with Him on intimate terms . . .

Give your children an opportunity to experience the anointing of the Holy Spirit . . .

And your children will crave the same spiritual nutrients as they grow up. Furthermore, they will never be able to point to a day in which they felt undernourished.

One day I was traveling with my family by car in Arkansas, and we were listening to tapes published by Hosanna. The words "Oh, the blood of Jesus" began to fill our car, and suddenly, I became aware that our twenty-nine-month-old daughter sitting next to me in the back seat was singing along, "Oh, the blood of Jesus . . . oh, the blood of Jesus." After two lines, our four-year-old joined in. They sang it from the bottom of their little hearts. Let me tell you, my heart was warmed. And beyond that, I know that the angels in heaven were rejoicing at their words.

Did our little girls mean those words? They sang them as if they meant them. They sang them with as much meaning as they say or sing anything else. True, they were mirroring the praise of their parents. Equally true, they were praising the Lord with their own lips. Simulation or reality? Both!

Your Goal
in Training

Your relationship with the Lord as a parent . . .
> Your relationship as a parent with your children . . .
> The relationship of your children with the Lord . . .
> Are to be seamless.

Your goal in training is not to create perfect children or to take imperfect children and create perfect adults. Your goal as a Christian parent is to bring your children to the point that they have a well-adjusted, intimate, and eternal relationship with Jesus Christ . . . every day of their lives, without a pause or break.

Training up your children to follow the Lord is the most time-consuming, most omnipresent, and most fulfilling activity you as a parent can ever experience. I encourage you to make it your foremost priority.

7

Training Up Your Children Through Discipline and Practice

Now therefore, listen to me, my children,
For blessed are those who keep my ways.
Hear instruction and be wise,
And do not disdain it.
—Proverbs 8:32–33

Many parents have said to me, "I just hope my children will meet God for themselves someday."

Meeting God isn't enough.

Children must be trained to serve God.

Knowing Jesus as Savior is not the same as serving Jesus as Lord. Serving the Lord is rooted in obedience, and obedience is a two-pronged effort: repeated presentation of what you want children to do, and chastening of children who willfully choose a different way.

The Importance of Repetition to Training

Not only do you train your children by example—by including them in the very things that make your own Christian walk meaningful and fulfilling as an adult—but you train them through repetition.

It isn't enough to have prayer with your children once a week or once a year or just once. Make prayer a daily habit in your family. It might be prayer at the conclusion of a family breakfast. Or a time of prayer before your children leave for school. Or the precious time of prayer with your children at bedtime. Make it the rare exception to miss an opportunity to pray with your children at least once a day.

If you travel and are away from your family a great deal, as I frequently am, you can still take time at the end of a day (or perhaps at the beginning of a day) to call home and have a little conversation with each child. Include in your conversation a prayer. Prayer knows no distance. It can be a deep spiritual tie that binds you to your children across the miles.

What is true for prayer is also true for repentance, praise, and giving. Instill in your children the principle that these behaviors are a normal part of living and that, in many cases, they are daily.

Yes, your children can ask forgiveness—and receive forgiveness—on a daily basis. Just as you insist that they take a bath every day and brush their teeth, you can help your children adopt a habit of asking the Lord to clean their hearts every day.

Yes, your children can praise God every day. There's much to be thankful for every day; there's always a reason to praise God for who He is—He changes not and is always worthy to be praised.

Yes, your children can give something to the Lord every day. It may be a praise offering. It may be an act of kindness. It may be a prayer offered for a loved one, a friend, an acquaintance, or even someone your children hear about on the news.

Habits are formed on a daily basis. Again, we must return to Deuteronomy 6:6–9:

These words which I command you today shall be in your heart. You shall teach them diligently to your children, and shall talk of them when you sit in your house, when you walk by the way, when you lie down, and when you rise up. You shall bind them as a sign on your hand, and they shall be as frontlets between your eyes. You shall write them on the doorposts of your house and on your gates.

You don't teach children the commandments of God once and then leave them to their own devices, interpretations, or self-willed behaviors. You are to train your children, or "teach them diligently." How? By talking about God's laws with them as a normal part of daily life. You are to continually point out God's laws at work—in nature, in human lives, in the problems and victories of the children's experiences.

Training children is daily work. It requires

• *constancy.* Your children need and rely on *always* knowing that you *always* love them and that your word is *always* your word. The same holds true for their relationship with God. They need to hear daily that you love them and that God loves them. Your children need to be able to count on you daily—to feed, protect, shelter, and nurture them. The same is true for God. Your children need to know that God's care for them is constant.

• *consistency.* Your children need to hear a message and to live with a code of acceptable behavior that they can rely on as being the same from day to day. Don't fluctuate in your demands about certain key principles of godly behavior. If it's wrong to steal on Monday, it should be wrong on Tuesday. If it's wrong to lie to a teacher, it's also wrong to lie to a younger brother. One of the foremost attributes of our Lord God is that He "changes not." Jesus Christ is the same "yesterday, today, and forever" (Heb. 13:8).

The constancy of God's love and the consistency of God's commandments are a great source of strength and confidence to your children. They form a spiritual foundation on which your children can gain firm footing. Knowing that God isn't going to change His opinion of your children . . . knowing that God isn't going to switch the rules of the game on your children . . . knowing that God's presence is eternal and His laws are fixed . . . give your children a sense of boundaries.

Although you may think your children want nothing but freedom, they actually *want* rules and guidelines. We all do. The freedom that we crave is the freedom to express our unique selves within God's parameters.

Four Things Worth Telling Your Children Every Day

The surest way to express the consistency and constancy of God is to let your children know again and again and again—as rhythmic as clockwork and yet always meaningful—that . . .

1. "The Lord Is with You"

Your children should hear this every day—as they go out to play, head to school, or face a challenge of some type. You may want to add, "I'm praying that His angels will continually surround you and uphold you."

Children today are exposed to so many types of superheroes. What a joy it is for them to sense that they, indeed, have superhero invisible allies on their side, none other than the heavenly host of the Lord God.

The story of Elisha and his servant in 2 Kings 6:13–23 is a good one to share with your children. The army of Syria had been sent to surround the city of Dothan, where Elisha had taken refuge. Elisha's servant went out in the morning and saw that the city was surrounded with horses and chariots. He came running back to Elisha, crying, "Master, what shall we do?" Elisha said, "Don't be afraid, for those who are with us are more numerous than those who are with them." And then Elisha prayed, "Lord, open his eyes that he may see." And immediately the young servant had a vision of horses and chariots of fire on all the mountains surrounding the Syrian enemy. Next, Elisha prayed, "Strike this enemy with blindness." And the Lord caused the enemy army to be blinded so that Elisha went out, talked to the soldiers, and led them off to Samaria, right into the heart of their enemy's land. When they realized what had happened, the leaders of the army were greatly humbled. After they shared a feast with Elisha, they returned to Syria and left the land of Israel in peace.

The truth of this story is a profound one to your children—God has a host of angels ready to fight on their behalf.

2. "The Lord Loves You"

The little song, "Jesus Loves Me, This I Know," is one of the first songs that a child should be taught:

> Jesus loves me, this I know.
> For the Bible tells me so.
> Little ones to Him belong.
> They are weak but He is strong.
> Yes, Jesus loves me.
> Yes, Jesus loves me.
> Yes, Jesus loves me—the Bible tells me so.

Even though it is considered to be a child's song, I sometimes find myself humming it. The meaning is no less true for adults. As far as I'm concerned, this song is a perfect lullaby for an infant. It should be among your children's primary memories.

Assure your children again and again that God's love for them doesn't change, and that nothing can separate them from God's love. Here are wonderful verses to read to your children frequently and perhaps even to write out and post where they can read them:

Who shall separate us from the love of Christ? Shall tribulation, or distress, or persecution, or famine, or nakedness, or peril, or sword? . . . Yet in all these things we are more than conquerors through Him who loved us. For I am persuaded that neither death nor life, nor angels nor principalities nor powers, nor things present nor things to come, nor height nor depth, nor any other created thing, shall be able to separate us from the love of God which is in Christ Jesus our Lord (Rom. 8:35, 37–39).

Even your children's disobedience doesn't separate them from God's love. It may position them for punishment, but it never separates them from His love.

Explain to your children the difference between loving a person and loving the *actions* of that person. You can dislike something that a person does but still love the person. That's an important distinction for children to see. You may punish your children for hitting a tennis ball through a neighbor's window after you have repeatedly warned them not to hit the ball in that direction. Your punishment doesn't mean that you love your children any less. In fact, your punishment is an example that you love your children enough to want them to grow up to be obedient, disciplined persons.

3. "God Hears You When You Pray"

Assure your children from the time they begin to talk that God hears them when they call out to Him. They don't need to use big words or even very many words. God sees the meaning of the heart, and He is always available to hear children's prayers and is quick to respond to them.

4. "God Wants Only Your Best, and He Promises to Give You Only His Best"

God is forever on your children's side. He wants to see them grow up to be His witnesses on the earth even more than you desire that. He has more faith in your children and in you as a parent than you sometimes have!

Your children cannot hear these statements about God's presence too many times. Make them a regular part of the encouragement you give to your children. They are foundation stones for spiritual development. Why? Because they point to God's eternal availability to His children. He is always there for us. Your children benefit by believing that every day of their lives. Intuitively, such a belief promotes in them a desire to always be there for the Lord.

The Need for and Value of Discipline

Repetition and discipline are closely aligned.

Spiritual discipline establishes spiritual boundaries, limitations, guidelines, and order for your children.

God has ordained an order of authority for the home. The apostle Paul wrote about this order in his letter to the Ephesians:

> Children, obey your parents in the LORD, for this is right. "Honor your father and mother," which is the first commandment with promise: "that it may be well with you and you may live long on the earth." And you, fathers, do not provoke your children to wrath, but bring them up in the training and admonition of the Lord (6:1–4).

The authority of a parent over a child is also reflected in the life of Abraham. Read what the Lord Himself said about Abraham:

> Shall I hide from Abraham what I am doing, since Abraham shall surely become a great and mighty nation, and all the nations of the earth shall be blessed in him? For I have known him, in order that he may command his

children and his household after him, that they keep the way of the LORD, to do righteousness and justice, that the LORD may bring to Abraham what He has spoken to him (Gen. 18:17–19).

Note the section, "He may command his children and his household after him, that they keep the way of the LORD."

As a parent, you have the responsibility for your children, and along with that responsibility, you have the authority for requiring that they follow after you to keep God's laws.

A parent doesn't have a blank check to require that children follow every whim or every abusive order. Your authority is based on this God-given premise: You follow and keep the ways of the Lord, and then you have the authority to command your children to follow after you.

That's also what the apostle Paul was saying when he said, "Fathers, do not provoke your children to wrath, but bring them up in the training and admonition of the Lord."

What provokes children to wrath? It's being ordered to do something that the parent does not do. It's being asked to obey a law that the parent disobeys, to engage in spiritual experiences (such as going to church) that the parent shuns. Therefore, require of your children only what you are willing to do. Don't punish your children for a messy room if your room is messy, too. Don't punish your children for losing their tempers if you are losing yours in the process! Chances are, *most* of your children's behavior is a mimic of your own!

You as a parent have the authority to command your children to follow in your footsteps only to the extent that you follow in the footsteps of Jesus. As you follow Him, you may require your children to follow you.

As you follow the Lord, you also have the responsibility

and authority to insist that your children stay within certain boundaries—those established by the Lord.

What is our number one boundary setter for parents as well as for children? It is God's Word. The Lord's highest desire is for us to do His Word always, in every area of our lives. Listen to this heart cry from the Lord: "Oh, that they had such a heart in them that they would fear Me and always keep all My commandments, that it might be well with them and with their children forever!" (Deut. 5:29). And again the Lord says, "Observe and obey all these words which I command you, that it may go well with you and your children after you forever, when you do what is good and right in the sight of the LORD your God" (Deut. 12:28).

To require that your children live within the boundaries of the Lord, you must first know them!

If you haven't thoroughly studied your Bible, make it a priority in your life to do so. It is the instruction manual God requires you to teach to your children. How can you teach it if you don't know it?

In many ways, your children are to be your disciples.

Long before the followers of Christ were called Christians, they were known as disciples. (See Acts 11:26.) A disciple is one who is being trained—disciplined. No place in the Scriptures do we find the option being given for a person to believe in Jesus and yet choose *not* to be a disciple. To be a Christian is to *be* a disciple of Christ.

Children are not exempt from discipleship.

They are to learn the Word of God primarily from you— through hearing the Word of God, being taught the Word of God, and having the Word of God lived out before them daily. Don't rely on your pastor or a Sunday school teacher or a youth group leader to take primary responsibility for teaching your children the commandments of God. That's your job as a parent.

Chastening Is
Part of Discipline

It is the privilege and responsibility of a parent to *insist* that children obey.

We have a dog, and the only thing we have trained our dog to do is to sit. Actually, our dog is not well trained because he sits only about half the time when he hears our command. The point is, when we say, "Sit," and the dog sits, he is exhibiting training. When he doesn't sit on command, he isn't exhibiting training.

Children are not dogs, of course. We can conclude, however, that when our children exhibit ungodly behavior, they are *not* trained in the things of the Lord. Proverbs 20:11 tells us, "Even a child is known by his deeds, whether what he does is pure and right."

When we realize that our children are *not* displaying Christlike behavior, we also must realize that they are *not* obeying the commands of God, and therefore, they are *not* trained up in the way they should go! At that point, we must make a concerted effort

• to intercede for our children with renewed vigor.

• to begin training them or continue training them in a more diligent, consistent manner.

The older the child, the more intense the intercession will need to be and the more difficult the training.

We really don't have the option before the Lord of writing off one or more of our children and saying, "Well, that one is the black sheep of the family," or "That one has a will of his own," or "We did our best, but that one just wouldn't obey."

Parents frequently say, "But I don't want to turn my children away. I don't want to alienate them. I don't want them so upset that they will run away or get into drugs or commit suicide." Parents who make these comments begin to tiptoe on eggshells around their children. They allow children to do whatever they will, and what they will is going to be manifest as rebellion. The children are likely to end up alienated from the parents.

Those are hard words, and I certainly am not condemning parents whose children have run away, become addicted, or committed suicide. I am saying that we as parents are not called to relate to our children under an umbrella of fear, including fear of what they may do. The spirit of fear is one that ultimately weakens, destroys, and kills. Rather, we are called and commissioned by the Lord to relate to our children in a spirit of love and discipline, and to insist that they obey and pursue righteousness as long as they live under our roofs. That is our role as parents as we chasten our children and provide discipline in following the commands of the Lord.

We can insist that our children obey the commands of God and that they show respect for the people of God—fellow Christians—especially for those in spiritual authority within the body of Christ.

One evening as I was concluding my presentation "Turmoil in the Toybox" in a church, a nine-year-old boy sitting on the front row led his friends in chanting "Turtles, Turtles, Turtles." He came up to me at the book table after the service and said boldly, "What you said about the Turtles is wrong! They're good!" I asked him if we could discuss the Turtles, but he refused. He turned and walked away abruptly. As he got to the door, he shouted back at me, "Anybody who says the Turtles are bad is a liar!"

That nine-year-old child will be eighteen years old in nine short years, and the disrespect he showed to me—not only as an adult but as a minister of the gospel—will be magnified a thousand times by the time he gets to that age. The disrespect will be solidified into a life-style and a refusal to accept authority and a refusal to accept as truth anything that doesn't line up with his personal view of the world. He is, in my opinion, well on his way to becoming a rebellious, self-centered, disruptive, and angry young adult, ready to blow away anybody in his path who confronts him.

In another incident, a six-year-old boy was standing next to his mother at the book table, and as she was preparing to buy the tape I had prepared on the Teenage Mutant Ninja Turtles, he said, "Oh, don't buy that thing. That guy is just stupid." I was standing just three or four feet away, and he knew it. The mother just shrugged her shoulders and put the tape back. (I wasn't upset that she didn't buy the tape; I was upset that she didn't correct the disrespectful behavior of her son.)

You may say, "Well, those are just examples of bad manners."

Yes, manners. Manners are a matter of respect. They are a form of godly behavior, showing preference to one another as described in Romans 12:10: "Be kindly affectionate to one another with brotherly love, in honor giving preference to one another." Manners are behavior. They are works. They are a manifestation of our faith in Christ and our willingness to hear out brothers and sisters in the Lord and then to compare their words with those of God's Word. Manners and a willingness to discuss things in the Lord are a reflection of God's behavior when He says, "Come now, and let us reason together" (Isa. 1:18).

Obedience to His heavenly Father and respect for humanity were the two great hallmarks of Jesus' life *from childhood.* "Then He [Jesus] went down with them and came to Nazareth, and was subject to them, but His mother kept all these things in her heart. And Jesus increased in wisdom and stature, and in favor with God and men" (Luke 2:51–52). Out of Jesus' obedience came wisdom. With wisdom came favor with God and people.

Obedience does not come *after* wisdom. It precedes it. Obedience is gained to a great extent through chastening of disobedience. We point toward obedience in all we do and say. And when what we do and say is not obeyed, we chasten with love. Proverbs 29:15 maintains, "The rod and rebuke give wisdom, but a child left to himself brings shame to his mother."

The one key qualifier for our chastening is that we administer it with *love.*

The writer to the Hebrews gives us a picture of how our heavenly Father chastens us:

"My son, do not despise the chastening of the LORD,
Nor be discouraged when you are rebuked by Him;
From whom the LORD loves He chastens,
And scourges every son whom He receives."

If you endure chastening, God deals with you as with sons; for what son is there whom a father does not chasten? But if you are without chastening, of which all have become partakers, then you are illegitimate and not sons. Furthermore, we have had human fathers who corrected us, and we paid them respect. Shall we not much more readily be in subjection to the Father of spirits and live? For they indeed for a few days chastened us as seemed best to them, but He for our profit, that we may be partakers of His holiness. Now no chastening seems to be joyful for the present, but painful; nevertheless, afterward it yields the peaceable fruit of righteousness to those who have been trained by it (12:5–11).

Notice the guidelines for discipline in this passage:

• Chastening is for the benefit—or "profit"—of your children. It isn't intended to hurt them; it is intended to train them and to bring blessing to them. It also brings the "peaceable fruit of righteousness." Chastening doesn't destroy the will or the creative spirit of your children; it molds that will and creative spirit toward the Lord.

• Chastening is to be done with a spirit of love, not anger. Do not punish your children when you are angry.

Wait to cool off and then approach them in a spirit of reason, compassion, and firmness.

• Disciplinary actions vary according to the person receiving the chastening. This passage points out that fathers chastened their children "as seemed best to them." Every child should be regarded as unique; chastening should be adjusted to the child. Ask the Lord to reveal to you the best way to chasten each child.

Have you ever trained a vine to grow on a trellis? The shoots of a young vine are tender and can be easily broken. If they are broken, they branch out, and you find that you have *two* shoots to train through the trellis. The more branching, the more difficult it is to intertwine the shoots with the latticework of the trellis. Therefore, a gardener takes special care in handling each tender young shoot, gently guiding it into position where it can become molded to the desired pattern. The goal is not to break or to bruise but to *guide*.

That is our role as parents as we chasten our children and provide discipline in following the commands of the Lord.

When you discipline your children . . .

• Let them know why you are taking the action you are taking. Tell them your goal—that they might grow up to be people the Lord can entrust with responsibility and blessings.

• Let them know on what basis you are requiring certain behaviors, and why the behavior you are punishing is wrong. Make certain that your children know clearly why they are being punished. You may even want to require that they express to you the reason for the punishment they receive. If a child has lied to you, for example, teach the child that lying is not acceptable behavior to the Lord God, and that is why it is not acceptable behavior to you. If you can't back up your punishment of an action with a word from the Lord, be very cautious. Make certain that you are not requiring more from the child than the Lord requires.

• Assure your children of your love. Point out to them the difference between your love for them and your disapproval of their actions.

• Enlist the power of the Holy Spirit. Ask the Holy Spirit to be with you as you chasten your children and to give you wisdom. As you discuss an incident with your children, watch for signs of repentance. If they apologize to you, accept the apology. (You may still mete out appropriate punishment, of course.) If your children desire to pray and ask the Lord's forgiveness for an action, recognize that desire and pray with them. (Again, that does not displace a punishment. Don't let your children use apologies or repentance to manipulate you out of taking an action that you believe the Lord would desire for you to take.)

Include Your Children in Christian Practice

In addition to simulation times of Christian behavior, such as confession, repentance, forgiveness, praise and worship, prayer, and giving . . .

In addition to repetition of key principles held out as constants for your children about the nature of God and their relationship with Him . . .

In addition to the chastening that enforces the principles of God in your children's lives . . .

Provide your children with practice times with other Christian believers. What do I mean by practice times? Opportunities to rehearse and develop corporate spiritual behavior. In other words, church as an event.

What is a church worship service?

Every worship service, to the extent that it truly is a

worship service, is a little foretaste of the day when we will join with all of the saints through the ages in crying "Holy, holy, holy" before the throne of almighty God.

What is a Christian marriage ceremony?

It is a sacred moment for two individuals who are committing themselves to carrying out a lifetime of Christian service and to raising up a Christian family. It is also a foretaste of the day when we, as the bride of Christ, are joined forever with Jesus in the marriage supper of the Lamb.

What is a Christian service of baptism?

It is an act of cleansing from sin and a mark on a person's life of being sealed as Christ's own forever. Baptism is an outward visible sign that someone has been birthed into a spiritual eternity from which the individual will never depart.

These and virtually all other sacred services and rituals of the church—virtually without regard to denomination or dogma—can be considered dress rehearsals for an eventual spiritual reality we will enjoy in the presence of our Lord.

They are practice sessions for us, preparing and equipping us for our work on this earth and, ultimately, our home in heaven.

Include your children in these experiences. They are the greatest training ground your children will ever set foot on.

We'll discuss this issue further in chapter 9, but for now, let me encourage you as a parent to

Take Your Children with You to Church

Don't shunt them off to a nursery so that they can play while you engage in the serious business of spiritual formation. Include your children in the process. They may not understand all that the pastor has to say. That's all right. They can't grow to understand what is said if they aren't present. If your children haven't developed a sermon-length attention span, take along a Bible puzzle book or Bible-based coloring book for them to work on during the sermon. Talk to your children later about the work they have done during church. You'll probably create a sermon in the process, one that they can fully understand.

It is in church that your children will become familiar with the great hymns and choruses that build up faith and give expression to our praise.

It is in church that your children will experience moments that truly reflect the beauty of holiness.

It is in church that your children will be able to observe others at worship. We all learn by watching and doing—appropriate church behavior included! Do your young children want to keep their eyes open during prayer times? Are they intent in watching other people pray or sing? Allow that to happen. It's the way they will learn.

If you attend a church where people clap along to the songs, let your children join in with the clapping. If you attend a church where people shake hands with one another in greeting, encourage your children to shake hands, too. If you attend a church where spontaneous individual prayer is the custom, encourage your children to pray, too.

Church services are practicums for your children. Full participation should be the rule, not the exception.

Notice, too, that I am encouraging you to take your children to church. Don't *send* them. Take them with you. Be a full participant.

Take Your Children With You to Other Church-Sponsored or Christ-Centered Events

Consider a family camp that may offer church services or training sessions as part of the daily schedule. Go to concerts of gospel music with your children.

Is your church sponsoring a special event with a missionary? Take your children along. They'll not only be fascinated with all that the missionary has to show and tell, but they'll encounter a way of serving Christ to which they might never have been exposed.

Many Bible-based training conferences or ministerial conferences now have children's programs that run parallel to the programs for adults. Check out the programs, and make certain that they truly provide spiritual nourishment. If they do, plan to attend as a family.

Don't leave your children at home with a baby-sitter while you seek a spiritual high point. Include them in the opportunity for spiritual growth and experience.

Include Your Children in Outreach Opportunities

Is a group from your church going to sing carols at a nursing home this coming holiday season? Take your children along!

Is a group from your church going to engage in witnessing at a major sporting event in your city? Include the children in your passing out of tracts or gospel literature. Let them be a part of the training sessions.

Why be involved in an outreach ministry as a family? Because it's important for your children to know that just one family can make a difference, in at least the life of one other individual. That knowledge builds in your children a sense of purpose, and that sense of purpose translates into a sense of fulfillment.

Count on the Holy Spirit to Help You with Reinforcement

For educational experiences to "stick" with children, they must be reinforced. That is, children must experience them in a positive and fulfilling way.

In the average educational setting, positive reinforcement is generally limited to praise or rewards—such as good grades, happy face stickers, or award certificates.

In the spiritual educational setting, reinforcement runs

much deeper. The result of good spiritual training is a deep sense of personal satisfaction and fulfillment in your children's lives. Another word for that is *peace*—not in the way we sometimes think of it but the deep shalom peace of the Bible. This peace is an abiding sense of wholeness. With it comes a great sense of personal value before the Lord.

The good news for parents as trainers of children is that the Holy Spirit has promised to be with us to reinforce what we teach.

Trust the Lord Himself to quicken the truths you impart to your children.

Trust the Holy Spirit to seal the good spiritual experiences to your children's lives forever.

Trust the Holy Spirit to confirm in your children's hearts the truth of the Word and the validity of the spiritual growth practices they experience.

Trust the Holy Spirit to guide your children as they explore their own means of prayer, praise, and giving. Trust the Holy Spirit to give good counsel to your children as they reach out to help others.

Trust the Holy Spirit to convict your children if they stray from the way in which you have trained them to travel.

Trust the Holy Spirit to reveal Himself to your children directly and wonderfully.

Trust the Holy Spirit to constantly nudge your children closer and closer to Jesus.

Trust the Holy Spirit to be with your children always.

Trust the Holy Spirit to fill your children with His presence and to give them the abiding sense of identity, confidence, esteem, and peace that only He can give.

The Holy Spirit is your coteacher in training up your children. Indeed, count on Him to be your teacher as a parent!

Ask the Holy Spirit daily for wisdom in how you should train up your children.

Ask the Holy Spirit to guide you and to reveal to you moments and experiences in which you can and should bring up the name of Jesus.

Ask the Holy Spirit to manifest His fruit in your life and to let your relationship with your children be one marked by harmony, communication, and love.

Ask the Holy Spirit to show you areas in your children's lives about which you can, and must, pray. Ask Him to reveal to you areas in which you as a parent can help fight a spiritual battle for your children's eternal sake.

Ask the Holy Spirit to manifest Himself through you to your children.

He has promised that when we ask for these things, He will provide them.

8

Sharing God's Word
with Your Children

From childhood you have known the Holy Scriptures, which are able to make you wise for salvation through faith which is in Christ Jesus.
—2 Timothy 3:15

"What should children be taught from God's Word? What parts of the Bible are best to teach them? Are there parts of the Bible that are directed to children?"

A man asked me these questions one day and started me on an exhaustive search of the Bible's references about children.

I discovered in my studies that only three or four stories in the entire Bible mention children in an allegorical sense. Virtually all of the references in which the words *child* and *children* are used can be taken quite literally to include or refer specifically to children.

In other words, the Bible is written about and to children in the very same way that it is written about and to adults. All parts of the Bible are aimed at children!

"But," you may say, "some concepts just seem too complex or deep for children."

Generally when that argument is raised, the issue involves big words, such as justification and sanctification, more than it involves difficult-to-teach concepts. Therefore, because parents have difficulty remembering or understanding the words, they assume that the concepts are equally difficult. Most children, however, can understand the meaning behind these "big words" if the meaning is given in terms they know—such as "being okay with God and acceptable to Him" or "being cleansed on the inside and set apart as God's special treasure."

Stop to consider the key concepts of the Bible that are the most meaningful to you. On your list may very well be

• holiness—a setting apart of one's life from the norms of this world in order to be used by God to bring redemption to this world.

• providence—the care of God over every detail and aspect of our lives.

• the will of God—God's plan and purpose for each human being.

• the fruit of the Spirit—the development within us of love, joy, peace, longsuffering, kindness, goodness, faithfulness, gentleness, and self-control.

Certainly among the basic concepts your children need to know are sin, redemption, grace, justification, and sanctification. Granted, they may not use these exact words, but they need to be able to express the meaning for these key Christian concepts in vocabulary appropriate to their age levels. Try these definitions with your children:

• *Sin:* Sin is what we do, and mean to do, that is wrong in God's eyes. When we sin, we hurt our relationship with God. Not only that, but our sin will destroy us in the long run. Sin hurts us. Sin may seem like fun for a little while, but eventually it will kill us. All of us are born with a nature that makes us want to sin. We need to ask God to take away that old nature, to forgive us for our sins, and to give us a new nature that will make us *not* want to sin. As long as we continue to hold on to our old natures, we cannot have a truly close relationship with our heavenly Father.

• *Redemption:* We get a new nature through redemption. God sent Jesus, His Son, to this earth to show us how to live a sin-free life. He died on the cross so that we don't have to die for our sins. In other words, He took our place on the cross and suffered the punishment that we should have received. When we believe in Jesus, and accept what He did for us, we are put back into a right relationship with our heavenly Father. He promises us that we can be free from sin, receive a new nature that doesn't desire to sin, and live with Him in heaven forever.

• *Grace:* Our being saved from sin is the result of God's work in our lives—His love given to us even while we were still sinners. We didn't deserve for Jesus to come and die for us, but God loved us so much that He made the first move to win us back. God chose to take the first step in restoring our relationship with Him, even though we were the ones who broke that relationship in the first place. God's work in our lives causes us to grow up spiritually and to become more and more like Jesus every day. We can't do that on our own. But we can invite the Holy Spirit of God to work in our lives and to cause us to grow.

• *Justification:* We are at peace with God when we accept what Jesus did for us and we choose to have a good relationship with our heavenly Father.

• *Sanctification:* God desires for His people to be separate from the evil of this world, to be thoroughly cleansed from evil, and to have no part in it. God's people are freed from sin so they might be used by God as His witnesses and agents on this earth.

I suggest that you take a long hard look at your list of key concepts most vital to your own Christian experience and then ask yourself, Are my children learning these concepts? Where? How?

Children Need to Learn More Than Bible Stories

Knowledge without power is dead. Yet much of what I see as children's curriculum—for home use as well as church use—is a presentation of factual knowledge about Bible stories.

Although having a general knowledge of the Bible's contents and being familiar with biblical stories are important, your children's spiritual education should begin at that point, not end there.

The way in which the majority of Bible stories are presented gives your children only "head knowledge." Most Bible stories are presented as bits of historical fact—a character is in a setting, takes action, and experiences results. Such stories are very similar to the social studies lessons that your children are given in school and over which they are quizzed with *who, what, when, where,* and *how* questions.

Your children need more than head knowledge about the Bible. They need to be equipped with the information and experiences that will truly make them young spiritual warriors.

Going for Key Principles

Your children need to be taught certain key principles that they can use on a daily basis.

Bible stories may be a good way to get into these principles, but be certain that the instruction goes beyond the facts of a Bible story to discuss its *meaning* and its *application* to your children's lives.

Let me give you an example.

Most children encounter the story of David and Goliath in the course of going to church or being read a Bible storybook at home.

The story is usually presented with this general story line, paraphrased here:

Goliath, a giant Philistine bully, has challenged the army of Israel. Everyone is scared to fight him. But David, a young boy, shows up on the scene and isn't afraid. He tells King Saul that he has killed a bear and a lion in the past while he was guarding his father's sheep, and he knows in his heart that he can take care of Goliath. King Saul tries to loan David his armor, but it doesn't fit and David decides to fight the battle his own way. He chooses five smooth stones from a nearby brook and, slingshot in hand, runs at Goliath. The stone flies from his sling and sinks into the only unprotected area of Goliath's body—his forehead—and Goliath is defeated. The Israelites win the battle. (See 1 Sam. 17 for the complete story.)

Ask children who have been to Sunday school for a few years to tell you this story, and chances are, they'll do a good job of spinning the yarn. Ask them what this story means, and they are likely to stare at you blankly.

What *can* this story mean to children?

First, it means that God has enemies. When someone comes against your children to try to destroy them or cause them great harm, that person is an enemy—not only of your children but also of God who loves your children. When someone takes on your children—whether to pick a fight or to issue abuse—that person is also taking on God. God is your children's ally in the battle from the very beginning.

Believe me, every child beyond the age of three years can understand this concept and find help and security in hearing this meaning attached to the story.

Second, the story of David and Goliath shows the great power of fear. The men in the Israelite army were scared of Goliath not because they had engaged in hand-to-hand combat with him but because he roared threats at them from a valley. Goliath looked scary and sounded scary. Fear kept the Israelites paralyzed. One great lesson in this story is that David refused to be scared.

That's a great concept for your children to see and learn. Young children often feel threatened by bigger kids. They understand from experience how fear can paralyze.

Third, the story defines when a battle is worth fighting and when it isn't. David clearly says, "Who is this uncircumcised Philistine, that he should defy the armies of the living God?" (1 Sam. 17:26). David isn't seeking his own personal revenge or glory. He is upset because Goliath is challenging the people of God. He is coming against God's people to destroy them. David tells the soldiers, "Is there not a cause?" (1 Sam. 17:29). In other words, "Isn't this a battle worth fighting?"

Children can understand that some battles are worth fighting and other challenges are worth ignoring. Children have an almost innate sense of knowing when a behavior is unjust or when it's just an annoyance. When Bob accidentally kicks sand in your face, a fight isn't necessary. When a group of kids bully a defenseless younger child into handing over his lunch money to them every day, a confrontation of some type is warranted.

Fourth, the story points to the fact that there are many different ways to win a battle. Goliath and King Saul knew of only one way: to don armor and go at it head-to-head with brute strength. David took a different course. He chose a method that *he* was good at. His way kept him mobile, with lots of maneuvering ability. He had the element of surprise on his side—Goliath was certainly not expecting to be downed by a stone from a slingshot, much less fight an upstart kid who came running down the mountain at him without any armor.

Children delight in this insight. Most children feel powerless because they are "little." Seeing that God has a way for even the powerless to win battles is greatly encouraging!

Fifth, the story illustrates reliance on God from start to finish in David's life. When David told King Saul about killing the lion and bear, he spoke of "the LORD, who delivered me" (1 Sam. 17:37). When David ran at Goliath, he shouted,

> You come to me with a sword, with a spear, and with a javelin. But I come to you in the name of the LORD of hosts, the God of the armies of Israel, whom you have defied. This day the LORD will deliver you into my hand. . . . The battle is the LORD's, and He will give you into our hands (1 Sam. 17:45–47).

The battle was won that day not so much by a slingshot and a smooth well-aimed stone as by faith. David knew without a shadow of a doubt that God was on his side. He trusted God explicitly to win the battle for him.

This concept is also one that children can understand. Faith is meant to be used—to be put into action. It means relying on God to do God's part, even as we do our parts. Children take confidence in knowing that God has a role and they have a role, and that together, they and God are a team.

Now, these are only five concepts that may be drawn from the story of David and Goliath. There are others, some of which may be more appropriate for older children (such as the fact that the stone didn't kill Goliath; David cut off Goliath's head with Goliath's sword).

Still, these five concepts alone build children's faith. They learn the facts of the story and insights into its meaning. Using this story, you can have a wonderful discussion with your children about

- what it means to be partners with God.
- how to face up to threats that cause fear.

• how to tell when someone is really coming against you to hurt you (versus someone who is just trying to get your attention or who is just trying to annoy you).

• the different ways that a problem might be solved.

• the importance of doing everything in life with faith.

• how to know when to fight and when not to fight.

• how to know which method of fighting to use in a battle.

Such discussions do more than give your children head knowledge. They cause your children to ponder the mysteries of God with a faith perspective and, thus, to grow spiritually.

Which brings us to the point of . . .

Getting to Application

A Bible story will remain hollow for your children unless it is applied to their lives in a very concrete, practical way.

Again, using the story of David and Goliath, you might ask them questions such as these as you read the tale and discuss it:

• Are you facing a giant today? Who is it? Why is this person an enemy? Do you think this person is also God's enemy? Why?

• Are you scared? What is the threat being made?

• Do you believe the Lord is on your side in this? What is He telling you to do?

• Do you have the faith to believe that God can bring you through this and take care of your enemy?

In discussing virtually *any* Bible story with your children, you might ask,

• How do you think the main character felt?

• Do you think this is the way you would feel?

• Do you think this is the feeling that Jesus would have? Is this a feeling that Jesus would seek to heal, or is it a feeling that He would join with you in having?

(By the way, these questions don't necessarily need to be limited to Bible stories. You can use them with totally secular stories, television programs, and videos to get at Bible-based spiritual truths and their application to your children's daily lives.)

Sealing the Message with Prayer

You may find it appropriate to conclude your time of discussing the principles and application of a Bible story in prayer.

If, for example, you have discussed fears and enemy giants with your children in an application of the David and Goliath story, pray along these same lines with your children. Talk to God together about the enemy your children face. Talk to God about the fear, and ask God to take the fear out of the children's hearts. Pray for the enemy. Ask the Lord to change the person's heart and to bring about justice in the situation. Ask the Lord to give your children assurance that He is at work in the situation and to show them evidence of a change.

Encourage your children to pray after you do. You'll probably be pleasantly surprised to hear that they mirror many of your words and phrases.

What is happening? Your children are being trained to fight a spiritual battle, just as David and Goliath fought a real battle in the Valley of Elah. Your children, counted as equal young warriors before the throne of God, are being equipped to handle a difficulty with faith in God.

Can you see the difference in children knowing *about* the story of David and Goliath and learning the story in such a way that it affects their lives and causes them to grow up in the Lord?

Yes, your children need more than a recitation of Bible stories. They need to be equipped and trained to become men and women of God.

Moving Beyond
Bible Stories

As important and prevalent as Bible stories are in the children's literature of the church, children need to discover that the Bible contains more than "stories."

As you give your children an understanding of the entire Bible, there are twelve key passages that I believe are vital to teach:

• The Ten Commandments (and the summary Jesus gave about the commandments)
• The Lord's Prayer
• The spiritual armor (as found in Eph. 6:10–20)
• A sequence of Scriptures about the need for forgiveness and about how to be born anew spiritually
• The Twenty-third Psalm
• The book of Proverbs
• A series of Scriptures that give your children a handle on how to deal with discouragement and fear
• The promises of God to His children
• The teachings of Jesus
• First John
• First Corinthians 12–14
• The death, resurrection, and ascension of Jesus

Let me offer some specific suggestions for sharing in each area . . .

The Ten Commandments

Your children should be familiar with Exodus 20:1–17:

> And God spoke all these words, saying: "I am the LORD your God, who brought you out of the land of Egypt, out of the house of bondage. You shall have no other gods before Me.

"You shall not make for yourself any carved image—any likeness of anything that is in heaven above, or that is in the earth beneath, or that is in the water under the earth; you shall not bow down to them nor serve them. For I, the LORD your God, am a jealous God, visiting the iniquity of the fathers upon the children to the third and fourth generations of those who hate Me, but showing mercy to thousands, to those who love Me and keep My commandments.

"You shall not take the name of the LORD your God in vain, for the LORD will not hold him guiltless who takes His name in vain.

"Remember the Sabbath day, to keep it holy. Six days you shall labor and do all your work, but the seventh day is the Sabbath of the LORD your God. In it you shall do no work: you, nor your son, nor your daughter, nor your male servant, nor your female servant, nor your cattle, nor your stranger who is within your gates. For in six days the LORD made the heavens and the earth, the sea, and all that is in them, and rested the seventh day. Therefore the LORD blessed the Sabbath day and hallowed it.

"Honor your father and your mother, that your days may be long upon the land which the LORD your God is giving you.

"You shall not murder.

"You shall not commit adultery.

"You shall not steal.

"You shall not bear false witness against your neighbor.

"You shall not covet your neighbor's house; you shall not covet your neighbor's wife, nor his male servant, nor his female servant, nor his ox, nor his donkey, nor anything that is your neighbor's."

In teaching these commandments of the Lord, you may want to shorten them, of course. This is the version I learned as a child:

- Thou shalt serve the Lord your God and Him only shall you serve.
- Thou shalt not bow down to any graven image.
- Thou shalt not take the name of the Lord in vain.
- Remember the Sabbath day to keep it holy.
- Honor thy father and thy mother.
- Thou shalt not commit murder.
- Thou shalt not commit adultery.
- Thou shalt not steal.
- Thou shalt not bear false witness against thy neighbor.
- Thou shalt not covet anything belonging to thy neighbor.

Now, I learned the commandments in the terminology and phrasing of King James's English, and I memorized them long before I had any understanding of the words *graven image*, *Sabbath*, *adultery*, *false witness*, and *covet*. In fact, I learned the words and their meanings as the result of memorizing the key principles.

What is the importance of these commandments to your children, who probably aren't in danger of breaking any of them except perhaps honoring father and mother? (You may want to explain to your children that *honoring* means "obeying, speaking well of, respecting.")

Primarily, it's the fact that God has rules and laws. He has established a way for us to live in relationship with Him and with other people. Furthermore, God expects us to keep His commandments, and He has sent His Holy Spirit to *help* us keep them and to put in our hearts a desire to keep them. He promises to bless those who do keep His laws and to punish those who don't. Above all, God has put these principles into effect *for our good*. The world would be a much much better place if everyone lived by these principles.

In addition to the Ten Commandments, share with your children the way Jesus summarized them:

> "You shall love the LORD your God with all your heart, with all your soul, and with all your mind." This is the first and great commandment. And the second is like it: "You shall love your neighbor as yourself." On these two commandments hang all the Law and the Prophets (Matt. 22:37–40).

Your older children can be taught the connection between the first three of the Ten Commandments and the first great commandment of Jesus, and the relationship between the last six of the Ten Commandments and the second great commandment Jesus gave. The fourth commandment is both an act of worship to God and a commandment for our personal benefit, a sign of loving ourselves.

As with the commandments of the Old Testament, the great commandments of Jesus are rooted in relationship. God desires above everything else for us to be in a loving, warm relationship with Him and a loving, warm relationship with other people. He gave His commandments to us as a way of making the relationships possible.

The Lord's Prayer

You can find this prayer in both Matthew 6:9–13 and Luke 11:2–4. Here is the version from Matthew:

> Our Father in heaven,
> Hallowed be Your name.
> Your kingdom come.
> Your will be done
> On earth as it is in heaven.

Give us this day our daily bread.
And forgive us our debts,
As we forgive our debtors.
And do not lead us into temptation,
But deliver us from the evil one.
For Yours is the kingdom and the
power and the glory forever. Amen.

Children as young as three years old can learn this prayer and recite it. It's a good prayer for your children to pray every day of their lives! As they grow, discuss various passages of the prayer with them.

What does it mean, for example, for the Lord to have said "Our Father"? What is critical for us to know about the Lord God as a Father? What does it mean for Him to be *our* Father as opposed to *my* Father? Why should we forgive our debtors? What does it mean for the Lord to deliver us from the evil one? What does it mean for His will to be done or for His kingdom to come on earth as it is in heaven?

Use this prayer as an opportunity to explore other areas of Scripture with your children.

Make it a recurring theme of your conversations with your children through the years. Their insight into this prayer, as with all passages of Scripture, will grow as they experience more of the Lord, have more experiences within the church and life in general, and understand more of God's Word.

The Spiritual Armor

The apostle Paul tells us about the "whole armor of God":

Finally, my brethren, be strong in the Lord and in the power of His might. Put on the whole armor of God, that you may be able to stand against the wiles of the devil. For we do not wrestle against flesh and blood, but against principalities, against powers, against the rulers of the darkness of this age, against spiritual hosts of wickedness in the heavenly places. Therefore take up the whole armor of God, that you may be able to withstand in the evil day, and having done all, to stand. Stand therefore, having girded your waist with truth, having put on the breastplate of righteousness, and having shod your feet with the preparation of the gospel of peace; above all, taking the shield of faith with which you will be able to quench all the fiery darts of the wicked one. And take the helmet of salvation, and the sword of the Spirit, which is the word of God; praying always with all prayer and supplication in the Spirit, being watchful to this end with all perseverance and supplication for all the saints—and for me, that utterance may be given to me, that I may open my mouth boldly to make known the mystery of the gospel; for which I am an ambassador in chains; that in it I may speak boldly, as I ought to speak (Eph. 6:10–20).

As you teach your children this passage of Scripture, have them act it out. Let them use hand and body motions to put the imaginary helmet of salvation on their heads, even as they say, "Take the helmet of salvation." Encourage them to dress themselves daily for spiritual battle.

Point out to your children that the purpose of this exercise is to be able to effectively stand up to evil. In putting on the armor of God, they are taking on the very nature of Jesus. They are saying, "I'm picking up the shield of faith," and "I have the shield of faith with me all day."

Teach your children how to use the armor when they come against difficulties or crises in life. Not only should they pick up the sword of the Spirit every day, but they should be taught that when temptations come, they can quote the Word of God to a situation—thus reminding themselves of the truth of God—and that in so doing, they will be resisting the enemy of their souls. When they resist, the enemy must flee.

Finally, point out to your children that this is a prayer. We put on the nature of the Lord in prayer, making it a top petition before the throne of God on a daily basis.

You may say, "I'm not sure my children can learn all this." Trust me. Your children *can* memorize this passage, and they will be grateful to have it as part of their readily recalled spiritual experiences when temptations come. I've heard a child as young as four years old recite this entire portion of Scripture without an error.

Salvation Series

Several verses are vital for your children to know, even to memorize. I've clustered them under four main headings.

1. *Everyone has sinned.*

There is none righteous, no, not one (Rom. 3:10).

For all have sinned and fall short of the glory of God (Rom. 3:23).

Whoever shall keep the whole law, and yet stumble in one point, he is guilty of all (James 2:10).

To him who knows to do good and does not do it, to him it is sin (James 4:17).

2. *Sin has consequences.*

For the wages of sin is death, but the gift of God is eternal life in Christ Jesus our Lord (Rom. 6:23).

The soul who sins shall die. The son shall not bear the guilt of the father, nor the father bear the guilt of the son. The righteousness of the righteous shall be upon himself, and the wickedness of the wicked shall be upon himself (Ezek. 18:20).

Of the tree of the knowledge of good and evil you shall not eat, for in the day that you eat of it you shall surely die

(Gen. 2:17). [Explain to your children that, in this context, the knowledge of evil refers to sin.]

Jesus said, "If you do not believe that I am He [the Savior], you will die in your sins" (John 8:24).

3. Christ made a sacrifice of His life for us.

For God so loved the world that He gave His only begotten Son, that whoever believes in Him should not perish but have everlasting life (John 3:16).

But God demonstrates His own love toward us, in that while we were still sinners, Christ died for us (Rom. 5:8).

For He made Him who knew no sin to be sin for us, that we might become the righteousness of God in Him (2 Cor. 5:21).

Nor is there salvation in any other, for there is no other name under heaven given among men by which we must be saved (Acts 4:12).

4. We are called to accept Christ's sacrifice.

Seek the LORD while He may be found,
Call upon Him while He is near.
Let the wicked forsake his way,
And the unrighteous man his thoughts;
Let him return to the LORD,
And He will have mercy on him;
And to our God,
For He will abundantly pardon (Isa. 55:6–7).

If you confess with your mouth the Lord Jesus and believe in your heart that God has raised Him from the dead, you will be saved (Rom. 10:9).

But as many as received Him, to them He gave the right to become children of God, to those who believe in His name (John 1:12).

If we confess our sins, He is faithful and just to forgive us our sins and to cleanse us from all unrighteousness (1 John 1:9).

Assure your children that they *can* make a decision for the Lord as children. They *can* know that they can confess Jesus as Lord, be fully pardoned by the Father, and be completely cleansed of all unrighteousness.

These verses aren't labeled "adult only" in the Bible. They are for all who love Jesus and seek to follow Him.

The Twenty-Third Psalm

The six verses of this psalm make up probably the most frequently memorized portion of the entire Bible:

The LORD is my shepherd;
I shall not want.
He makes me to lie down in green pastures;
He leads me beside the still waters.
He restores my soul;
He leads me in the paths of righteousness
For His name's sake.
Yea, though I walk through the
    valley of the shadow of death,
I will fear no evil;
For You are with me;
Your rod and Your staff, they comfort me.
You prepare a table before me in the presence of my
    enemies;
You anoint my head with oil;
My cup runs over.
Surely goodness and mercy shall follow me
All the days of my life;
And I will dwell in the house of the LORD
Forever.

161

This psalm gives great comfort not only to adults but also to children. Children have enemies, too. Children get tired, too. Children need goodness and mercy to follow them. Children want to know that they will dwell in the house of the Lord forever.

Young children who memorize this chapter at an early age will be able to benefit from it all the days of their lives.

Proverbs

Read the entire book of Proverbs again and again with your children. You may want to read a verse every day with them as a part of your breakfast time. Many of us give our children vitamins to supplement their diets. A proverb-a-day is a supplement to all of the other spiritual food your children should be receiving.

The first nine chapters of Proverbs are often called proverbs to youths. They include such admonitions as:

My son, hear the instruction of your father,
And do not forsake the law of your mother;
For they will be a graceful ornament on your head,
And chains about your neck (1:8–9).

Incline your ear to wisdom,
And apply your heart to understanding;
Yes, if you cry out for discernment,
And lift up your voice for understanding,
If you seek her as silver,
And search for her as for hidden treasures;
Then you will understand the fear of the Lord,
And find the knowledge of God (2:2–5).

Trust in the Lord with all your heart,
And lean not on your own understanding;
In all your ways acknowledge Him,
And He shall direct your paths (3:5–6).

The LORD by wisdom founded the earth;
By understanding He established the heavens;
By His knowledge the depths were broken up,
And clouds drop down the dew (3:19–20).

Let your eyes look straight ahead,
And your eyelids look right before you.
Ponder the path of your feet,
And let your ways be established.
Do not turn to the right or the left;
Remove your foot from evil (4:25–27).

Go to the ant, you sluggard!
Consider her ways and be wise (6:6).

The commandment is a lamp,
And the law a light (6:23).

Have you noticed how concrete the proverbs are? These verses tell of necklaces, treasures, paths, clouds, eyes and eyelids, ants, and lamps. Children relate in a special way to concrete things. The proverbs paint visual pictures that children can "see" and understand long before they know the meaning of all the words.

Make your children familiar with the book of Proverbs. Reading it again and again through the years will ingrain its principles in your children's minds.

Discouragement and Fear

Two of the most potent verses you can teach your children are these:

For God has not given us a spirit of fear, but of power and of love and of a sound mind (2 Tim. 1:7).

Lo, I am with you always, even to the end of the age (Matt. 28:20).

The Lord is, indeed, with us . . .

And His gift to us is His presence, which is of power, love, and a sound mind . . .

We therefore have what it takes to stand up to fear and discouragement.

Read the first chapter of the book of Joshua with your children. Set the stage. The children of Israel were about to cross the Jordan River after forty years of wandering in the wilderness. They had been set free from bondage in Egypt and were about to claim what God has said would be theirs. At the same time, they were facing battles. The Promised Land was occupied. Three times in this chapter, we find this phrase: "Be strong and of good courage" (vv. 6, 9, 18). In verse 7, we read, "Only be strong and very courageous." These are good words to instill in your children.

One of the best defenses against discouragement and fear is to alert your children that persecution *will* come. The Lord never promises us a walk in the park—only that He'll be with us as we walk!

Isaiah conveys these words of the Lord:

Listen to Me, you who know righteousness,
You people in whose heart is My law:
Do not fear the reproach of men,
Nor be afraid of their insults.
For the moth will eat them up like a garment,
And the worm will eat them like wool;
But My righteousness will be forever,
And My salvation from generation to generation (51:7–8).

It is normal and natural for every human being to experience fears related to survival. We can count on the devil attempting to instill other fears in us—fears that are not of God and are not natural. They are fears to be withstood in faith. Two of the foremost fears the devil attempts to plant in us as parents, and in our children, are the reproach of men, which brings a loss of prestige, status, or reputation, and a loss of material possessions.

This great promise from the Lord tells us, however, that those who bring these fears against us are our enemies, and that He will destroy them. God's promise is that His righteousness will live forever, and that His salvation will be manifested from generation to generation.

In a very practical way, these verses provide you with ammunition against peer pressure that might try to pull your children away from faith in God. You can let your children know, on the basis of these verses, that peer pressure is going to come. People will speak negatively about them and tease them and accuse them of all kinds of silly and untrue and damaging things. The fact of God, however, is that He promises to sustain them and to save them from the taunts and threats and to give them a place with Him forever.

What do peers generally use as a weapon to drive a wedge between your children and the values of your home? Fear. A fear of being teased, separated, called names. That's the "reproach of men." Its purpose is to make them scared of losing face, losing their status, losing their reputation among others whom they like and with whom they want to associate.

The second fear is the fear of loss of or damage to something children have or are—perhaps loss of milk money or damage to a bicycle or a black eye or the threat of not being able to get home without being hurt. These are the "insults" of men.

Most of the threats are never carried out—they are just that, threats rooted in fear. Arm your children with an awareness of the enemy's tactics against them. Let them know that the Lord promises to be with them.

God's Promises

Your children need to know that God has made certain promises to those who believe in Jesus Christ and who follow in the Way established by Him.

Here are seven passages that will give your children great hope for the future:

Jesus spoke to them again, saying, "I am the light of the world. He who follows Me shall not walk in darkness, but have the light of life" (John 8:12).

Behold, I stand at the door and knock. If anyone hears My voice and opens the door, I will come in to him and dine with him, and he with Me. To him who overcomes I will grant to sit with Me on My throne, as I also overcame and sat down with My Father on His throne (Rev. 3:20–21).

Therefore, if anyone is in Christ, he is a new creation; old things have passed away; behold, all things have become new (2 Cor. 5:17).

If you abide in Me, and My words abide in you, you will ask what you desire, and it shall be done for you. By this My Father is glorified, that you bear much fruit; so you will be My disciples (John 15:7–8).

Again I say to you that if two of you agree on earth concerning anything that they ask, it will be done for them by My Father in heaven. For where two or three are gathered together in My name, I am there in the midst of them (Matt. 18:19–20).

Judge not, and you shall not be judged. Condemn not, and you shall not be condemned. Forgive, and you will be forgiven. Give, and it will be given to you: good measure, pressed down, shaken together, and running over will be put into your bosom. For with the same measure that you use, it will be measured back to you (Luke 6:37–38).

You are the children of the LORD your God. . . . For you are a holy people to the LORD your God, and the LORD has chosen you to be a people for Himself, a special treasure above all the peoples who are on the face of the earth (Deut. 14:1–2).

These verses proclaim to your children that they *can* live victorious lives in Christ. They *are* worthy before the Lord, and they *do* have a purpose on this earth. Their prayers *can* be answered.

The Words of Jesus

Purchase for your children's use Bibles in which the words of Jesus have been printed in red. Focus their attention on those words. Express to them the importance of knowing what Jesus said as a way of establishing a deeper relationship with Him. Jesus invites us to speak and do His word, to speak it to our generation and to live it out in our daily lives. To speak and do His Word, we must first know it!

The First Letter of John

This is a wonderful love letter. When your children feel discouraged, rejected, or disappointed, suggest that they read this book. A teenager will take about fifteen to twenty minutes to read all five chapters.

First Corinthians 12–14

These three chapters teach your children how to balance the use of spiritual gifts with love. All children need to know that they are "gifted" by the Holy Spirit. The gifts are not something to be proud of; they are gifts to be sought, cherished, guarded, and used for the benefit of others.

I believe 1 Corinthians 13 is a chapter that all children should be encouraged to memorize. It's a wonderful passage to mold a loving nature within them. Make it a part of their prayer lives to request from the Lord these attributes of love.

The Death, Resurrection, and Ascension of Jesus Christ

Not only at Easter, and perhaps especially at times other than Easter, the chapters of the New Testament telling of Jesus' death, resurrection, and ascension have special meaning for children.

In Matthew, I suggest you begin with chapter 21. It tells of the triumphal entry into Jerusalem and includes some key teachings of Jesus during His final week before the Crucifixion.

In the gospel of Mark, begin with chapter 11, again with the triumphal entry. The story in Luke begins in chapter 19, verse 28.

In the gospel of John, I suggest you begin with chapter 11, the raising of Lazarus, which is the event that sparked the triumphal entry. Chapters 14–17 give us Jesus' last major message to the disciples, including His wonderful prayer for them. John 14 is another chapter worthy of committing to memory.

Explore Your Children's Interests

Beyond these basic Scriptures, encourage your children to pursue subjects that are of interest or benefit to them such as the following:

• Subjects related to reports they are researching for school

• Hobbies or personal interests

• Animals, birds, and fish

Encourage your children to dig out this information for themselves. Don't do the Bible study *for* them. Instead, let them research a Bible study and give it to you!

One of the best studies you can encourage your older children or teenagers to pursue is a study of what the Bible says about money.

I grew up learning many wonderful things from my parents, but I did not learn how to handle money. My parents didn't willingly or knowingly choose *not* to teach me about money; they simply didn't. Only as an adult did I realize that Jesus never went to the bank to get a loan for His ministry; He didn't pull out a credit card to finance His trip across the Sea of Galilee. I know I am not the only child who grew up in the 1950s and 1960s not knowing how to manage money. I suspect I'm part of an overwhelming majority.

Your children need to know what God has to say about money.

Your children need to know what the Bible has to say about sex, marriage, and fidelity. You may need to explain some words for them. Be sure your children see that a sexual relationship in marriage and procreation are wonderful gifts from God.

These and other studies of the Word of God are easily pursued if you show your children how to use a concordance. A good question to ask is this: "I wonder if the Bible has anything to say about that?"

Underscore the Absoluteness of God's Word

Let your children know that you regard the Bible as the "absolute" word from God. The Word

• is not negotiable. We can't barter with God over His laws.

• is to be taken in its entirety. We aren't allowed to pick and choose the parts we like and discard the rest.

• is to be applied to life. We aren't just to "know" God's Word. We're to live it out.

Viewing God's Word as absolute and vital provides for your children a solid defense against deception.

The foremost trick of the deceiver is to attempt to twist God's Word, to misapply it, or to take it out of context. Alert your children to these tricks up front.

Above all . . .

"Salt" Your Communication with Scriptures

As a parent, one of the best ways you can instill the Word of God in your children is to use the Scriptures as part of your conversation. Memorize and then quote to your children key verses of importance to you. Make them a normal part of your conversational habit. Can't you envision how such statements might be used in everyday life?

• "Isn't that great? It's a real example of 3 John 2 that God wants us to prosper and be in health."

• "Wow, that's a real example of Proverbs 22:24 isn't it —'make no friendship with an angry man.' "

• "I shouldn't have had that second piece of pie. Mark 14:38 is really true—the spirit is truly ready, but the flesh is weak."

Include Scripture, too, as you pray. Use it to remind yourselves of God's promises and His presence as you pray. Use it in standing against the enemy. Use it to build your faith to believe God will provide what you need and will answer your petitions in His way and timing.

Help Your Children Memorize Key Verses

The Scriptures encourage us again and again to hide the Word of the Lord in our hearts where it will remain a ready and sure resource for us. Jesus Himself said, "The kingdom of heaven is like treasure hidden in a field, which a man found and hid" (Matt. 13:44).

Encourage your children to memorize key Bible verses. They can do this by

• reading the verse over and over again—perhaps as many as a dozen times.

• breaking the verse down into key phrases and memorizing each phrase, then stringing the phrases together.

• reciting the verse aloud to themselves a number of times during a day or week.

In some cases, a verse may need to be simplified for young children. Always urge your children to learn the "address" of a passage—book, chapter, and verse. That way, they will know where to go later in life to read the verse in its entirety or to discover more about its context.

Express to your children the reason to memorize Scripture: so that they might use it! Scripture is meant to be learned so that we recall it later and give voice to it as we

• remind ourselves of God's truths when we face decisions or feel doubt.

• speak encouragement to ourselves in times of persecution or danger.

• seek to share the good news of Jesus Christ with someone in need or someone who desires to enter into a personal relationship with the Lord.

• engage in spiritual warfare. The Bible promises us that when we recite the Word of God to our spiritual enemy, he will flee. (See the example of Jesus facing the tempter in the wilderness [Matt. 4:1–11].)

As your children learn a Scripture and commit it to memory, discuss with them how and when such a verse might be used. Anticipate in advance a situation or circumstance in which the verse might bring comfort, counsel, or victory. Give your children a reason to add the verse to the spiritual arsenal.

What About a Family Bible Study Time?

I will be candidly honest with you about what I have witnessed of family Bible studies—sometimes considered a vital part of a family altar time. Generally speaking, these times are advocated as a set time each night or once a week when families stop what they are doing and gather together for Bible reading and prayer. Many people suggest family altar times as a "must" for spiritual growth and bonding in a family. I do not.

From what I have seen, these times usually take on a sense of obligation, and in most cases, they have an unnatural, "meeting" feel to them.

Now, if you can institute a set time in your family in such a way that it is natural and has spontaneity and life . . . if you can create a time every day that is something you and your children look forward to . . . I heartily encourage you to do so. If, however, it becomes drudgery to you and something that your children dread, find another way.

Prayer at bedtime is natural for my family and me. A few minutes spent with each child talking to the Lord bonds us together. At other times, I enjoy sitting down with my children and reading Bible stories to them and discussing them. But for the most part, these are unstructured times that arise naturally and spontaneously.

My father was a wonderful preacher. I'd put him up against any preacher in this nation. But when he and Mom instituted a family devotional time, it was sheer boredom. My brother and I felt like pulling out toothpicks to hold our eyelids open.

Even on Christmas Eve, my brother and I found the traditional family reading of the Christmas story—that beautiful loving story—to be boring. My brother and I *knew* that it should be a special time. We wanted it to be.

But it was never truly as wonderful in reality as we wanted it to be in theory.

The good news is, my father soon realized that the daily devotional time was not the process that would pass his faith on to my life.

Some of my favorite memories are of the time my father was the pastor of one of the largest churches in southern California—a position that demanded nearly every waking hour. I was in elementary school during that pastorate, and my father made a decision that his role would be to fix breakfast for the family and then drive my brother and me to school. Those breakfasts and rides to school were times for sharing. I knew that I could always count on those times with him. I didn't realize until much later that my father wasn't just being a nice guy. He was using those hours to teach us things of God and to talk with us in a natural day-to-day way about the power and working of God.

All of Our Lives
Before the Altar

I did learn from my father's example that *all* of life could be lived before God's altar. We didn't need to stop what we were doing as a family to invite God's presence into our home. He was already in our home and in all our doing.

Every family is different and has its own general rhythm, temperament, and schedule. In our home, Cynthia and I find it more of a burden to try to schedule a family devotional time with three children under the age of seven than to attempt to have periodic one-on-one conversations with each child about God's Word.

Our favorite times of sharing God's Word with our children are times when we spontaneously sit down to read to our children from their children's Bibles, play Bible-based games with them, or read Christian storybooks to them. We use these warm, close, child-centered times as opportunities to interject Bible principles. For the most part, these moments are unstructured; they arise naturally.

If our children want to leave the story midway and move to another activity, we allow it. If they want to stop and ask questions or skip to the end, we allow that. They'll get the whole story, and all of the principles, in the course of many unstructured, spontaneous readings. And it will be in doses that they can accept and digest spiritually.

I advocate strongly that we train our children to read and study the Bible on their own and to pray on their own. I believe these activities are far more valuable than a set family Bible study time for two reasons:

• First, an independent relationship develops between your children and the Lord.

• Second, you, as a parent, are allowed to grow in your relationship with the Lord at your own depth and pace.

Your children need to see you reading your Bible. They must see you in times of personal Bible study and in prayer. They will hunger to do what you are doing, especially as they perceive it to be crucial for your life. And they will imitate your pattern.

In so doing, they will discover for themselves the richness of God's Word and the joy of prayer.

On the other hand, if they come to rely on you, as the parent, or on the family as a whole to do the praying, reading, and studying, an individual reliance on the Lord will never develop.

How can you instill this practice in your children?

Try turning off the television set, grabbing your Bible, and sitting down with it for an evening of personal reading and study. Invite your children to get their Bibles and do the same. You might even tell them what passage you're going to study. Tell them you'd like to hear their insights into God's Word. And see what you will learn that evening from them. I guarantee you it will be far more beneficial to all of you than an evening of prime-time programming!

The Word Is
for Our Benefit

As a final word . . .

Encourage your children always to see the Word of God as being *for their benefit.* God has given us the laws, promises, miracle stories, and parables as a means of building up our faith so that we might live victorious, prosperous, whole lives.

Let your children know that you regard the Word of God as life giving.

Children always seem to look forward to mealtimes. Instill that same love for God's Word in them as a time for spiritual nutrition and joy.

9

Finding a Church That Puts Your Children First

There was not a word of all that Moses had com-
manded which Joshua did not read before all the
assembly of Israel, with the women, the little ones,
and the strangers who were living among them.
*   —Joshua 8:35*

I've heard untold num-
bers of speakers say, "The children are the church of tomorrow." I disagree. Our children are not the church of
tomorrow—they are the church of today! If we do not
count them as the church of today, there will not be a
church of tomorrow—at least not one with our children as
members.

Let me point out to you something you might not have
considered.

Your children will spend the equivalent of six days in
church this year if you attend every Sunday for an average
length of service. Your children, if they are "average Ameri-
can children," will spend the equivalent of forty-four days
this year in front of a television set.

What do television producers assume about your children that church leaders generally fail to assume?

Television producers assume that your children will be
influenced by messages about products, make a choice to

want a product, and then bug Mom and Dad into making a purchase on their behalf. Television producers assume that your children have buying power, even though they don't have any money.

Church leaders, on the other hand, are more likely to assume that your children can't consume the Christian message or experience. They assume that your children can't be influenced by the message or make a choice about accepting Jesus Christ as Savior and Lord. Furthermore, church leaders tend to assume that your children can't influence an unsaved parent or loved one to make a similar decision.

Television producers assume that your children can and will experience television programs in a way that will make them want to watch more and more television programs.

Church leaders, however, frequently assume that your children will "burn out on God" if they are exposed to too much church experience.

Television producers know that your children are sexual, spiritual, and energetic beings. They appeal to your children's fleshly instincts with a wide assortment of fast-paced titillating, occult, and violent symbols and behaviors.

Church leaders, however, often assume that your children's spiritual nature will remain in an embryonic state until some magical age of accountability and, therefore, do very little to appeal to their need for a deep spiritual relationship with their Creator.

Jesus never made such assumptions. He not only ministered to children, He made ministry to them a priority.

Let the Children
Come to Jesus

Matthew records a relevant incident:

> Then little children were brought to Him that He might put His hands on them and pray, but the disciples rebuked them. But Jesus said, "Let the little children come to Me, and do not forbid them; for of such is the kingdom of heaven." And He laid His hands on them and departed from there (19:13–15).

The people longed to bring their children to Jesus for a touch, a blessing, and the disciples began to run interference. They valued the Lord's time too much. They saw the children in the same way that the culture at large viewed children at that time—as undeveloped, unworthy, unimportant, unqualified humanity.

And Jesus denounced the disciples for attempting to keep the children away from Him. He said, "Let them come. Don't stand in their way."

Let's recognize the context of this scene. Jesus has just spent an intense time in ministry. As any preacher will be quick to tell you, ministering is draining. The preacher who gives his all under the anointing of God comes away from that time of ministry emotionally and physically exhausted. That's the situation Jesus is in.

Furthermore, Jesus knows that when He feels that way, the best thing to do is to withdraw for a time of restful fellowship with His heavenly Father. He has already told the crowd and His disciples that He is withdrawing to be alone for a time of prayer.

And at this most difficult moment the children come.

Does Jesus say to the children, "I have already dismissed the service. Come back another time"? No. Does Jesus say, "Listen, I have more important things to do. I'm going now to spend time with God the Father"? No. Does Jesus say, "Listen, I'm exhausted right now. Let me catch up with you when I'm feeling refreshed and have some energy"? No.

Are you aware that the only example in the New Testament of Jesus being delayed in His ministry is this occasion when children were brought to Him?

Jesus *delayed* His plan to focus His attention on children.

Jesus *postponed* for a few minutes or hours a prayer encounter with His Father to lay His hands on the children and bless them.

Jesus was a man in control of His ministry. Only the children received ministry from Him *on their terms.*

We must face this critical fact. Jesus paused for children. They *became* His priority. They captured His full attention. They interrupted His schedule. And He not only allowed it, but He rebuked people who tried to stand in the way of the children.

We adults so often become irritated when children interrupt our agendas, schedules, or services and demand our attention. Let's make Jesus our example. He stopped what He was doing, delayed where He was going, and gave the children His full attention when they came to Him.

In your own home, when a child comes to you needing the touch of Jesus that only you can give to that child, stop what you are doing—put everything else on hold—and touch that child. Answer her question about the Lord. Listen to her insights into God's world. Hug and hold that child in need. Pray with the child who is hurting. There's no more important task you can accomplish than to be the hands and arms and mouth and ears of Jesus to that child in that moment.

We must take children on their terms and in their timing. Children live in the immediacy of a moment, and if we fail to respond to them on their demand, we miss critical opportunities.

Feeding the Lambs

In preparing His disciples for ministry, Jesus also gave top priority to children.

Consider Jesus' last words to Simon Peter—ones given during a lakeshore breakfast meeting just shortly before His ascension. Jesus asked Peter, "Simon, son of Jonah, do you love Me more than these?" He said to Him, "Yes, Lord; You know that I love You." He said to him, "Feed My lambs."

Twice more, Jesus asked Simon, "Do you love Me?" Each time, Simon said, "Yes, Lord; You know that I love You." The second and third times, Jesus replied, "Tend My sheep," and "Feed My sheep." (See John 21:13–17.)

This scene is one of the most dramatic in the New Testament. Simon Peter, who had denied the Lord three times, was being asked to confirm his love for the Lord three times. Simon Peter, the great fisherman, was being transformed into a good shepherd.

As a fisherman, Peter's relationship to the fish was a simple one: haul in the fish, keep the big ones, and throw the little ones back into the lake. Oh, what a picture of what happens in many of our churches today! How many altar calls are aimed at adults. The bigger the fish, the more we want to see them saved. We *like* to keep the big ones and throw the little ones back into the lake to grow up.

But that wasn't the order of service the Great Shepherd gave to Peter, the would-be shepherd. He began His command to Peter with the words: "Feed My lambs."

Start with the little ones. Nurture them. Be with them from the beginning of their lives. Protect them from the enemy. Rescue them when they go astray. Cause them to grow up.

The good shepherd knows that if the lambs are not fed, the flock will eventually die. Jesus called Peter to lead a church that would not die but would flourish. His first order of business was to tend the "little ones," the new lambs of the faith.

Children First!

The conclusion we must draw is that if Jesus made time for the children and considered them His top priority . . .

If Jesus admonished Peter *first* to care for the little ones . . .

Then we as parents must do our utmost to get our children involved in a church that follows Jesus' example and commands.

Imagine for a moment parents who decide to go out for a wonderful five-course dinner at the best restaurant in town. They seek an experience that is not limited to the food. They want "atmosphere," too—a nice decor, beautiful music in the background, candlelight, those who will be quick to meet their needs. They use the occasion not only to eat but to talk—to share from the heart and to communicate with the loved one. They're willing to pay for this experience, and if all goes as they anticipate, they will return home several hours later happy and physically stuffed.

Meanwhile, they probably have hired a baby-sitter for their children, and their children have probably dined on take-out fast food.

Although there's nothing wrong with doing this in the natural world from time to time, there is something desperately wrong about doing it spiritually, especially in making it a spiritual pattern.

And yet, isn't that what many of us have done? We hear that Brother Wonderful is holding a series of meetings and our first thought after "Let's attend" is, "Who can we get to watch the children?"

We go to church where we enjoy a good meal of God's Word, warm fellowship with our fellow saints, and ministry that meets the needs in our lives—complete with beautiful decor, lovely music, and sometimes candles—and we send our children downstairs to be watched over. While we feast, our children are given the spiritual equivalent of junk food.

It is not just an injustice. I firmly believe it's a sin before God. We owe it to our children to affiliate with a church that meets their needs.

Let me share with you six qualities I believe you need to look for in a church home.

Church Quality 1:
Find a Church Where the Pastor and Church Leaders Seek to Serve Children First

The first persons we must serve in our churches are the children.

This notion goes against the grain of what most pastors or church workers desire to do.

Young children don't have anything to contribute financially to the church.

Children are energetic and demanding. They want only what works. They don't like substitutes or imitations of the real thing. They want something with life, and they don't settle for meaningless messages.

Children *are* harder to minister to than adults. That's mainly owing to their attention span. If children have a five-minute attention span, the person ministering to them needs to switch gears to gain their attention every five minutes. Rather than a three-point sermon, a minister needs to have a three-phase program. It's doable, but it's more difficult. I won't kid you about that.

Children don't stroke the egos of those who minister to them. They don't line up at the exit door of the Sunday school class and say, "That lesson was such a blessing. I don't know how I'd make it through the week without you as my teacher."

Children can't express what *doesn't* meet their needs.

Consider for a moment an adult Sunday school class in which donuts and coffee are offered every Sunday morning —and then comes the morning when the donuts and coffee disappear. Can't you hear the response? Several will no doubt say, "Where are the goodies? I paid my tithes. These things ought to be here." A few will say, "I'll guarantee you one thing, there *will* be donuts and coffee next week." A couple may even go out of the room in search of donuts and coffee or at least to find someone to collar about the situation in order to register a complaint.

What is likely to happen the next week? There will be donuts and coffee in that room and probably better donuts than have ever been there before!

Consider now the room designated as a Sunday school classroom for the three-year-olds. The air conditioner goes out. The three-year-olds become just as hot, sweaty, and irritated as their adult counterparts would become. Their normal attention span is cut in half. They begin to cry.

Is any change made in this room on the basis of what the three-year-olds do? Not likely. The situation will be remedied only if an adult gives voice to the problem.

The difference? The children have no power to effect change.

In areas of spiritual growth, a second related problem exists. Children simply don't know what they might be missing.

Should a group of mature Christian adults begin to feel that they are no longer being properly fed the Word of

God, they are likely to confront this fact and seek a solution—ideally, by discussing it with the church leaders rather than by dropping out of sight and going to the church down the street.

What about a group of five-year-olds, however? They have nothing against which to gauge their spiritual growth or the diet of spiritual food they are being fed. They don't know what they might be missing.

These are just two areas in which adults *must* become advocates for children. You, as a parent, must choose a church where the children are placed first and fed the spiritual food they need in an atmosphere that shows them respect. The children cannot make this choice for themselves.

The Benefits Are Too Good to Miss

What do you gain, however, by making your children the top priority in the church?

First, children always challenge you to be more like Jesus. Every time you minister to children, they challenge you to be more like our Savior and Lord. They challenge you to have the kingdom of God working in you because that is the only way they can begin to experience the kingdom of God.

One of the most wonderful traits about young children is that they don't pretend when it comes to church. They love to see God at work and to feel His presence, but they don't pretend He's there when He isn't. They "feel" God, and they know when they feel God that it is God they are feeling!

Do you want a good evaluation about the work of the Holy Spirit in a service? Ask children, "What was the best part of that service to you?" Nearly without fail, they will pinpoint the times in the service when the Spirit of God was felt the strongest—it might have been during a Communion service, the choir's song, an altar call, or the singing of a great hymn or praise chorus. (Unfortunately for many of us who preach, children may or may not include the sermon as the high point of the service spiritually.)

Furthermore, children aren't full of doctrines. They don't filter the church experience through a series of expectations about what should and shouldn't be said or done. They haven't developed a lot of "surely he doesn't mean me" or "I know that so well I can ignore what is being said" responses to the Word of the Lord, whether it's presented through the reading of Scriptures or the preaching of a sermon. Children, thus, are actually far more open than adults when it comes to receiving the full impact of an anointed message or song or to hearing "with ears to hear" a new insight into Christian living.

If you want to make room for the manifestations of the Holy Spirit of almighty God in your midst, you must make room for the children to participate in His presence. Children long to experience the Lord's presence, and the Lord desires that they have this intimacy with Him.

Second, the way in which your church ministers to the children will directly affect the anointing that rests on the remainder of that church's programs. How is this so?

If the children in your church are not trained to be obedient to the Lord—truly trained to be truly obedient to everything the Holy Spirit desires to do in and through their lives—the *opposite of obedience* is established. There are only two options: obedience or disobedience. Another word for disobedience is *rebellion*. Rebellion opens up people to the work of the enemy, not the work of the Holy Spirit. In fact, it shuts down the capacity of the Holy Spirit to work.

When rebellion is a primary force within a church, the Holy Spirit cannot be manifested in the fullness of His glory and power. Jesus Himself could do no mighty works in an area where He found no faith, which is another way of saying "rebellion against the things of God."

"But," you say, "we're talking about children."

In a typical church in our nation, approximately one-third of those in attendance on any given Sunday are children. Stop to think about your church. Factor in all of the children who are downstairs or who are missing. For every two adults present, there's likely to be one child somewhere within the building (or a child who *should* be within the building).

When one-third of the congregation are not being trained for obedience to the Lord and are thus in disobedience . . . a spirit reigns that limits the anointing of the Holy Spirit.

Third, a priority ministry to children puts your church in a position for growth and prosperity. In my travels over the past decade to literally thousands of churches across our nation, I've come to a clear awareness that those churches emphasizing family life are the ones growing—both in numbers and in depth of spirituality.

Show me a church where children are made welcome, and the nurturing and training of children to become mighty men and women of God are made priorities, and I will show you a church that is growing—usually, quite rapidly.

Such a church invariably attracts unsaved, unredeemed families. It's as if the warmth and love expressed for the children are contagious. Unchurched parents see in the children, in the families, and in the very church itself something that is almost mysteriously but unmistakably attractive. They want their children to be part of such an atmosphere and to experience a relationship with God as generous and loving Father. In becoming a part of such a fellowship, their own lives are subject to renewal, and with the renewal of the parents' lives, the commitment to church membership grows even stronger. A new family is added to the church rolls and to heaven's rolls.

That family in turn touches the lives of other un-churched families, and so it goes. When the children are put first, the church's population explodes! Churches that honor children and make them a priority are churches that are not growing one by one. They are churches that are growing family by family. And friend, that makes for exponential growth.

At the same time, the church that puts children first is a church that becomes intentional about such concepts as these:

- the development of the mind of Christ.
- the nurturing of children toward holiness.
- the involvement of children in praise and worship.
- full citizenship for children in spiritual matters.

A church with that mind-set is the best possible place for new converts to be! The new converts are instantly made to feel welcome in spiritual gatherings. Their praise and worship are regarded as valuable and appropriate. Their development toward holiness is encouraged. Their development of the mind of Christ in their lives is fostered through educational programs and Bible studies.

The fact is, all persons come into the kingdom the same way—they are "born" into it. All persons grow up in their faith the same way—as children growing toward maturity.

A related phenomenon in these churches that honor children is financial prosperity.

People give when they see results that touch their lives personally. When a father and mother see their children blessed and their family begin to grow and develop a spiritual maturity, they *know* the reality of the church's ministry in a very real day-to-day way. They *want* to support such a church. They are eager to attend and get involved.

They want to see others reached so that they can experience the blessing they have come to know. And giving begins to grow exponentially.

Are you in a dying, lifeless church today?

Get this book for your pastor and mark these pages. Tell him you are willing to work with him in whatever ways he desires to see the training of the children in your church made a top priority. And then see what the Lord will do.

I once was in a church where the pastor stuttered very badly. It took him a couple of minutes to introduce me, and all he was trying to convey was my name!

The second time I ministered in that church, I asked a church leader, "How is it that your congregation stays so faithful to someone who has such great difficulty communicating? I admire this tremendously, but I am also amazed."

The man said to me, "Have you noticed in your visits here that sixteen key leaders of this church carry out the day-to-day ministry?"

I said, "Yes, I've noticed that."

He said, "Have you noticed that they are all the same age—in their early thirties?"

"Yes," I said, "I've noticed that."

He continued, "In the ninth grade, those sixteen people were in the same room of this very church, and the Spirit of God came upon them. From that day to this, they could not do anything else *but* serve God and serve Him as a team. I know, because I was one of those teenagers."

I said, "How many people attended your church before that time?"

He said, "About 120."

"How long had that been the size of your congregation?"

He said, "Oh, about twenty years."

Today, that church has a thriving, alive, growing congregation of more than two thousand in attendance.

What made the difference? Certainly the faithfulness of the pastor in creating an environment where young lambs could be fed. Above all, it was the work of the Holy Spirit in the lives of young people who were in ninth grade—about fourteen or fifteen years old!

Fourth, a church that places a high priority on children tends to be a church marked by energy, exuberance, and joy. I have yet to be in a congregation that placed top value on the salvation and equipping of children with spiritual tools that did not radiate the joy of the Lord.

That perhaps is the greatest hallmark of churches in which children are given top billing. An exuberance of these churches and an enthusiasm for the things of God are contagious. As a visiting minister, I can feel both the minute I walk in the door.

When, on rare occasion, I find myself invited to a church that seems "dead on arrival," I usually look around for the children, and I invariably find them missing. When the children are absent, so is the overflowing joy of the Lord. Oh, you may find it in an individual or two, but the general feeling of the congregation is one of staleness.

By the way, I believe these same principles of prosperity and joy relate directly to the family, too.

Consider the position of the Lord. He sees a family raising children to love and serve Him, and He can look ahead and see that any inheritance the children receive is going to be used with generosity for the growth of His kingdom.

On the other hand, if the Lord sees a family raising children who will not love and serve Him, He can look ahead and see that any inheritance given to the children will be used in a way contrary to His kingdom.

It is what you give of good—what you give of the Lord—that becomes good seed. The Lord multiplies the good seed.

Families that bless their children and put them first are

families that are multiplied in their provision and, above all, in their joy. The Lord releases warmth and love and enthusiasm for life into such a family.

I've talked to many people raised in such homes who were not rich in money or material possessions, but without exception, those people felt rich. They thought they had a great overflowing abundance. They felt no lack or want that was painful to them. Instead, they look back— sometimes on quite impoverished childhoods—and they say, "I was so fortunate. The love and fellowship in our family were so great. The presence of the Lord was real to us. I wouldn't trade my childhood for anything."

I have concluded without doubt: A spirit of prosperity and a spirit of joy accompany the training of children in the ways of the Lord . . . both in the church and in the home.

Yes, you *owe* it to your children to find a church where *your children* are number one citizens.

Church Quality 2:
Find a Church That Desires to Teach Its Children How to Live Victorious Lives

Find a church that teaches your children

• how to withstand persecution (especially from peers).

• how to discern the will of God (through confirmation of a word by Scripture and other believers, through a "quickening of the heart," and through stepping out in faith).

• how to walk by faith (trusting God on a daily basis for direction, guidance, and provision).

In the church, we have tended to focus on salvation— the experience of receiving Christ into one's life—and in many cases, we have dropped our concern at that point. The fact of the matter is, however, that even though persons receive Jesus Christ into their lives, they must then develop the mind of Christ, or the salvation experience will not manifest itself in day-to-day activities, decisions, and behaviors.

To have the mind of Christ is to take on Christ's ethical behavior. We must begin to do things the way Jesus would do them if He was living in our day. We must be able to pray daily, "Help me, Lord to do this . . . help me to say this . . . the way that You would say it."

Doing what Jesus would do, and saying what Jesus would say, is the basis for our integrity as Christians. It's matching what we believe with how we act and speak. It's matching what He has done for us with how we will live for Him.

Many people have had a salvation experience and yet have not gone on to develop a Christlike ethical basis for the way they live. They have not taken on the mind of Christ or adopted His way of life as their own. The result is that although they may profess Christ with their lips, their actions reflect the world's pattern of situational ethics. When hit with a crisis or a problem, they tend to deal with that problem in the same way a nonbeliever would deal with it. They revert to the world's standards for behavior rather than reflect Christ's behavior.

The *greatest* challenge we face with our children is not getting them to the altar to pray a sinner's prayer. Our greatest challenge is leading them to develop the mind of Christ so that they become new creatures apart from the world's system.

Our Christianity is intended to have a twofold manifestation to the world: behavior and belief. Unless they are both present and working in harmony, our Christian witness falters, and indeed, Christ is not fully at work within us. Our belief—our faith—falters and is inconsequential or dead if it isn't linked to behavior, or works. Works without faith have no eternal value. "What does it profit, my brethren," asks the writer of the book of James, if someone says he has faith but does not have works? Can faith save him? If a brother or sister is naked and destitute of daily food, and one of you says to them, "Depart in peace, be warmed and filled," but you do not give them the things which are needed for the body, what does it profit? Thus also faith by itself, if it does not have works, is dead. . . . For as the body without the spirit is dead, so faith without works is dead also (2:14–17, 26).

Works are the way in which we deal with the natural, physical world around us. Works are practical. They are behaviors and deeds. They very often have a tangible aspect to them. When we read in Proverbs 22:6 —"Train up a child in the way he should go, and when he is old he will not depart from it"—we read words that apply to the natural, physical world in which we live. We train a child to do works—to exhibit a certain pattern of behavior, to deal with life in a particular way.

This comixture of belief and works so vital to victorious Christian living will come about only if the church you choose to attend encourages children, *as children*, to *experience* the spiritual reality of a living, vibrant relationship with the Lord and a daily walk based on a Christlike ethical code.

I have a suspicion that some parents don't share the reality of a living faith with their children because their own impression of religion is that it's boring. I agree with them 1,000 percent. Religion *is* boring. Religion is dogma, ritual, and rules.

A relationship with God the Father, Son, and Holy Spirit, however, is anything but boring!

Please recognize one vital fact. Such a relationship does not happen automatically through church attendance alone.

Involvement in church activities, in and of itself, does not automatically result in your children having a solid spiritual relationship with the Lord. For example, children may participate in a youth choir for two years without missing a practice session and still feel nothing of the presence and power of God. I find it better, of course, for children to be singing songs about Jesus than eating pizza and going bowling under the guise of youth group activities. Still, the true youth program will be marked by these characteristics:

• It is bathed in prayer by those who lead it.
• The leaders will have as their ever-present, overriding purpose the training up of children to love and serve the Lord.
• The leaders will continually seek ways in which the Word of God can be creatively communicated to the children.
• The children or teens will come away from the experience better equipped to live their lives for the Lord and to feel more of God's presence and power at work in their lives on a "twenty-four-and-seven" basis—twenty-four hours a day, seven days a week.

In most cases, going out for pizza together doesn't involve any of these characteristics. At best it provides an opportunity for a Christ-centered conversation. Even given that, unless the leaders are intentional about such a conversation taking place, and are highly motivated to guide such a conversation and to bring forth results from it, the conversation in all likelihood won't happen.

Some of the most notorious self-proclaimed sinners of our age were children who grew up in church without ever experiencing spiritual reality.

Aleister Crowley called himself the beast; painted the numbers 666 on his forehead; was an avowed bisexual; believed he could cause others to become demon possessed; and stated as his goal in life to break every moral and spiritual law in existence. He grew up the son of a Plymouth Brethren minister.

Hugh Hefner, founder and publisher of *Playboy* magazine, the man who made pornography popular, grew up in church.

Alice Cooper, the man who preached satanism as a natural extension of youthful rebellion, and who embodied some of the most violent, despicable, and repulsive behaviors ever enacted on the rock and roll stage, grew up in church, attending every Sunday and Wednesday.

Salina Fox runs a witchcraft training center in Wisconsin. During a commercial break on a television interview program in which we were both guests, she said to me, "Phil, your God is too small." I responded, "Salina, your god is taking you to hell." She said, "Oh, I know all about what you preach and believe. I grew up the daughter of a Baptist deacon."

Also during that program, eight people in the audience stood and announced, "We're witches, and we're Christians, too." One woman said, "I've experienced more spiritual reality in neopaganism than I ever did in the Methodist church where I grew up." Another said, "I have a master's degree in theology. I can teach in your Bible schools and colleges. I believe Jesus Christ was a witch who performed His magic through the use of elemental spirits."

Let me tell you something, those eight people are sorely confused and in danger of losing their souls.

Still, they point to a very real circumstance: The world and the devil will provide for your children a compelling case for social inclusion, spiritual power, and group acceptance.

Unless your children have been raised to know what they believe and where they stand in the Lord on the basis of their *own* involvement and experience with the Holy Spirit and with fellow Christians who actively love and serve the Lord, they will be easy prey for an agent of Satan who says, "I have something you want." Indeed, it *will* be something your children want initially. In the long run, the power offered to them and the group that accepts them will kill them, in reality or spiritually forever.

Church Quality 3:
Find a Church in Which the Youth Minister Feels Specially Called to That Role

In many churches, the youth minister is simply a new minister. Youth ministry is considered in some denominations almost to be the bottom rung of the corporate ladder. After a few years of youth ministry, a person might become an assistant pastor and then move on to be a pastor.

What does this line of succession tell you about the value placed on youth ministry? If the youth minister is simply "putting in time," the person won't be giving a 100 percent effort as unto the Lord.

In still other churches, the primary youth workers are volunteers or even draftees. I can't imagine a situation in which a pastor would ask the congregation if there were any volunteers to preach the sermon on Sunday morning. Yet, that is frequently the case in children's church programs. Those who lead children's worship experiences must be more than mature, willing, doctrinally sound adults who love children. All of these traits are vital, yet not sufficient. Those who minister to children must have a divine calling and anointing for just that work. (See 1 Cor. 2:4; 1 Pet. 4:11.)

Find a church in which the youth minister understands the spiritual warfare she faces.

Perhaps the most intense battle in the heavenlies is the battle over our children. Children who come into youth programs from homes in which the parents are not diligently seeking to train their children for Christian faith and service will bring a spirit of ungodliness into a youth meeting.

This spirit is often manifested as an attitude of cynicism or an attitude that what is about to happen in the service is unimportant, inconsequential, or unreal. The result is a lack of attention and, generally speaking, disrespectful behavior.

If this spirit is not broken, little will be accomplished. The entire meeting may well degenerate into a goof-off session.

A youth minister who is truly called to this office will pray and prepare himself intensely for a meeting. He will not feel a need to be one of the kids but will know that he bears a spiritual responsibility for these lives before the Father. He will be able to exercise true spiritual authority and not allow anything to disrupt the work of the Holy Spirit.

A youth minister who truly feels called to that area of ministry will not seek to entertain your children.

I once spoke on a Sunday evening in a large church in one of our major cities—a church with more than three thousand members and a full-time youth minister on the staff. The responsibility of the minister included providing a special program of ministry for those four years old and younger during the regular worship service.

She went to my wife after the service and said, "I showed this to the children while your husband was speaking. I hope it's okay." And then she handed her a copy of the videotape *Cinderella.*

The children—the little lambs of that church—were given a diet of Disney while their parents were given a diet rich in the Lord's Word.

That was not an isolated instance. In fact, in many places, keeping the children occupied with entertainment goes on while adults are in worship services.

Not long ago I was invited to speak at a national convention. It was a day session and the only session of the convention for which a children's program hadn't been arranged. The announcer advised the more than one-thousand-member audience, however, that if they wanted to take their children to a room that had been reserved to the side of the main hall, the children would be watching four videos while I spoke. When I was given the microphone a few minutes later, I said, "Will someone please go to my book table at the back of the auditorium and take four of the Christ-centered videos we are offering to the room where the children are? At least they'll be watching something about Jesus while I speak."

When my wife went into the room to see what they had intended to show the children, she discovered that among the videos scheduled were *Bedknobs and Broomsticks*—a Disney feature movie about witches with abundant occult overtones—and *Roger Rabbit* with all of its vulgarity.

Friend, Disney is no substitute for spiritual training.

Entertainment Is a Cheap Substitute for the Real Thing

Let's consider for a moment what the enemy is doing. Around the world, even as you read this book, he is preparing children for combat and for world domination. Children are being trained to use automatic firearms on the streets of our cities and in distant jungles and rice paddies. Children are being taught to march and to recite the tenets of their belief—whether the words of Marx, Mao, or Muhammad. Children, especially Mormon and Jehovah's Witnesses children, are being sent out on missions with their leaders. Children are being trained to defend their turf and change their world through whatever violent methods are necessary, generally so that an evil ideology can win.

What are we doing in the church?

More of our children are playing than preparing.

In many of our churches, children are being entertained during church services rather than being trained in intercession, evangelism, and the deep truths of the Word of God.

This issue is worth discussing a little more thoroughly.

What do you expect as an adult when you go to church? From my conversations with men and women in hundreds of congregations across this nation, I've concluded that *most* men and women go to church expecting three things to happen:

• *to experience God in some way—to feel His presence, His love, His forgiveness.* Even if persons aren't seeking an intensely emotional experience, they usually want a sense of inner satisfaction that they have done something pleasing to God, and that when they leave the doors of the church building, they are in right relationship with the Lord.

• *to hear God's Word proclaimed and to be inspired by it.* Most people want their faith reinforced and renewed. They want a "charge" of God's Spirit to propel them into the next week.

• *to learn something about living the Christian life that they can apply immediately.* Most people want a faith that will mean something Monday through Saturday. They want to know that Christianity makes a difference, and that it can work for their ultimate good.

Secondarily, adults go to church because they enjoy the fellowship with their friends or want to give something of themselves (whether ushering, teaching Sunday school, or putting an offering in the plate when it passes by).

What do many—indeed, I believe most—of our children expect when they go to church? A good time.

We have entertained our children in church so much that they have come to expect to be entertained. A video. A puppet show. A craft exercise. A time of playing.

Take a peek into your local church youth area—from nursery up to age ten—and tell me it isn't so!

Why do we think our children *don't* want the same things that we want as adults?

I believe we've convinced ourselves of three great falsehoods.

First, we tend to think that children can't experience what we experience in church They won't understand the sermon, they won't be able to sing the hymns, they won't be willing to sit still that long, and therefore, they won't get any meaning from the church experience.

I categorically disagree with this premise. Young children experience a service at an intuitive, spiritual level, even if their young minds can't comprehend all of the words being spoken or sung. Soon, the children *will* be singing along—usually, even before they can read music or the lyrics! Soon, they *will* be joining in as the congregation prays.

I once watched a three-year-old sit through an entire sermon without fidgeting. What captured his attention? The play of light coming through a beautiful stained glass window. He was utterly fascinated by the changing colors and the way in which the rays cast a rainbow on the opposite wall and on various segments of the congregation.

Did that child have a spiritual experience at church? I believe he did. I believe that a wonderful sermon about light was planted in his spirit, one that he will recall later in life when he listens to sermons about Jesus being the light of the world, the importance of our being light to our generation, and the nature of light expelling the darkness. He might also have gained insight into the beauty of holiness and perhaps even an intuitive understanding of how Jesus can "refract" Himself into all of our lives simultaneously. I don't know, of course, that the child took in all this meaning. I do know that the look of awe on his face said that something wonderful was happening inside him. And I trust the Holy Spirit to be the One who was creating that wonderful moment.

The premise, however, that children can't experience what we experience in church leads to a related falsehood . . .

Second, we tend to think that children need a different presentation of the gospel from what we need The prevailing opinion seems to be that children need Bible stories and act-out choruses. Although children may enjoy a rousing rendition of Daniel and the lions' den, once they have heard that story a few times, they know it and can probably recite it with more energy than most of the adults who will tell it to them.

Let's not sell our children short. They can understand more than Bible stories. They can appreciate music that doesn't have hand and body motions. They can and they do relate to anointed preaching, healing services, and prayer services.

Third, we tend to think that children need to "like" church so that they will want to keep coming. Therefore, since children "like" to be entertained, we entertain them so they will want to keep coming back Although it is true that children like to be entertained, our responsibility as parents is not to entertain them in church. Our responsibility is to prepare our children to love and serve the Lord, to grow up spiritually, and to learn to use the weapons of spiritual warfare.

Children will eventually realize—and sooner than most of us like to think—that they can be entertained in at least a dozen ways that don't involve getting up and getting dressed on a Sunday morning. Entertainment is virtually universal in our culture. It's available at the turn of a knob in our living rooms. It's as near as the toy chest. It's nonstop. Why, then, go to church to be entertained?

Let's face it. The world can entertain our children far better than the church ever can. Rather than try to compete, let's try a radical alternative. Let's regard the church experience as an opportunity to prepare children to live out Christian principles at school and on the playground, to withstand persecution from their peers, and to win souls for the Lord.

Closely related to the idea of entertainment is the notion of developing church friends. Again, the thinking seems to be that if children have friends at church, they will want to attend.

If the main relationship at church is a social one with peers, children quickly realize that such a relationship can be duplicated elsewhere without nearly as much effort or constraints. Friends abound. Why hang out with kids at church when you can hang out with kids next door?

In trying to keep our kids interested in church by entertaining them and socializing them, we actually give them the very "out" that most of them choose to take: leaving church to spend time at leisure pursuits with their friends.

And yes, I meant it when I wrote that is the out most of our church-raised children are taking. I recently read a survey reporting that 75 percent of the children in one mainline denomination leave the church between the ages of thirteen and eighteen. Of those who leave, about one in four returns to that particular denomination later in life. About one in four begins to attend another denomination. Half remain outside the church. Half of the initial 75 percent results in 37.5 percent of these children, raised faithfully in a mainline denomination, leaving the church and not returning. I consider that a major hemorrhage.

I suspect, however, the real reason we don't want our children in a worship service with us is *not* nearly so well thought out. I suspect the real reason is that we simply don't want to be bothered by the presence of children.

Children do cry in church. They also cry at home just about as frequently, by the way.

Children do sometimes talk out loud. Actually, children have very few other occasions in their lives when they must communicate by whispering.

Children do sometimes fidget. So do adults. There are few occasions in our culture in which we are asked to sit absolutely still for the length of time required by some sermons.

Many parents find that they cannot concentrate on the worship experience for themselves because they are spending so much time controlling or watching the behavior of their children.

My contention is this—children will learn how to behave in church only if they are *in* church. Believe me, children who are shuttled off to a children's hour are not being taught to whisper, avoid crying, or sit still in that setting.

What About Misbehavior in Church?

I have a very basic belief about children's ability to behave in church that I would like to share with you: I believe they *can* learn to sit quietly during an entire church service. Children learn to do this in the same way they learn all other appropriate behaviors—through repetition and discipline. It is a matter of *training*.

What should you do when children misbehave in church? Take them out, discipline them, and bring them back into the service.

If you need to do that ten times in one service, do so. Within a matter of two or three church services, you will likely have no more problem. Don't believe me? Try it and see.

A big problem arises, however, if you take children out of the service and let them play outside the service or take them to a nursery where they can play with toys and, generally speaking, do their own thing. In essence, the children win out. They have their way. They have succeeded in exerting their will over yours.

Children who are taken out, corrected, and brought back into the service quickly catch on—I *must* be here, and if I don't want to suffer consequences I don't like, I *must* behave.

This leads me to yet another key concept regarding church behavior and church attendance . . .

Parents have the right to insist that their children attend church with them and behave during a church service. I'm continually amazed at the number of adults who don't seem to think that they have any right to require certain behaviors of their children. You do have that right! Furthermore, you have that responsibility before the Lord.

You can require that your children—even your teenagers—go to church with you, and that once there, they behave in an appropriate manner.

By the way, in some cases, rebellion against church attendance can be as simple as a dislike for dressing up. If so, that's an easy nonspiritual matter to deal with. Don't force your little boy to wear that stiff-necked, bow-tied outfit or your little girl to wear a hat and ruffles. Let the children be comfortable. It's a shame to let itchy, uncomfortable clothing stand in the way of your children hearing and partaking of the gospel!

Some parents seem to be unwilling to reinforce appropriate church behavior with disciplinary actions because they don't want their children to associate church (including God, Jesus, the faith, and so forth) with a negative reaction. That isn't the message being reinforced! The message reinforced to children is that misbehavior is not allowed in church because it is inappropriate to show disrespect to the Lord and His people.

Explain to your children as a part of your chastening

that you simply will not allow irreverent behavior in church because of your respect for the Lord. He is our Savior, the Divine Majesty, the object of our worship. We are quiet in church out of respect for Him.

Likewise, we do not exert our wills during a church service. We are there to experience *His* working in our lives. For God to work in our lives, we must be open to His working, and that requires a reverential attitude.

Finally, we are respectful to others in church because they are part of our spiritual family. We owe them the same courtesy we would like to receive.

I once heard a father say in disciplining his young son, "Your mother and I, and all the people around us, can't hear God over your crying. Stop your fussing. We are in church to hear what God has to say." I found that a fairly straightforward, simple answer that was not only theologically sound but easy for the child to understand.

Yes . . .

Children can learn to sit still in church. Children can engage in alternate activities that are still spiritually enriching during a sermon. Bible-based coloring books, puzzle books, or storybooks are great time occupiers.

I know of one family that allowed the children to look through or read only their children's illustrated Bibles during the sermon. On most Sundays, the mother of the family would point out to each child the passage in the Bible from which the pastor was speaking. The children had a wonderful time during the sermons—thinking about and imagining the reality of the stories behind the beautiful illustrations in their Bibles, reading the Word for themselves, and becoming familiar with the books of the Bible and where they could be found. The sermon time certainly wasn't wasted. And as the children became older, they found themselves listening more and more to the sermons.

You may say, "Aren't these activities also a substitute

for the real thing? Why should children read a Christian storybook or a children's Bible—or work Bible-based puzzles—when they can be downstairs in the church basement hearing a Bible story being read?"

The difference is twofold.

First, children who occupy themselves with a Bible-related activity during a sermon are still *in* church, and they are being prepared for full participation in that setting. The storybook substitutes only one part of the total experience, not the entire experience. It is an appropriate activity *very similar* to a sermon event.

Second, children are actively engaged in the process. There's a great deal of learning difference between reading a story for yourself and having one read to you.

The importance of this suggestion really lies in the content of the material you choose for your children during the sermon time. I once saw three children coloring Teenage Mutant Ninja Turtle pictures during a church service. I could hardly believe my eyes. Their parents had actually given them stories to color that were based on a cartoon series noted for its violence and its occult symbols, and that has its foundation in a theology (which ninja is, by the way) 100 percent contrary to Christianity.

I have also seen a number of other time occupiers that I would never recommend: little girls playing with dolls during a church service, little boys running small cars along pews, children reading non-Christian comic books.

When choosing a sermon-occupier activity for your young children, choose something that edifies and builds up. Make the activity or booklet a sermon substitute of as near like value as you can!

And start and stop the activity with the sermon. Don't let your children engage in the activity for the entire service. The time of the sermon in a service is for edification and proclamation that Jesus is Lord. Make certain that this time for your children offers the same opportunity.

All of these suggestions are made, please understand, as a second-best alternative, primarily because I recognize that not all sermons will hold children's attention. That's not a put-down to preachers. It is a recognition that most preachers do not preach to children or do not preach sermons at a level in which children can understand them.

The ideal situation is for children to give 100 percent of their attention to the sermon. Certainly by the time they are eight or nine, they should be required to do this, regardless of the quality of the sermon.

You can enhance this process in several ways.

First, make it a point to discuss the sermon with your children later in the day—perhaps over Sunday lunch. Ask questions about the sermon, such as:

- "What about the sermon hit you the hardest?"
- "What did you learn from the sermon today?"
- "What questions did the sermon raise in your heart?"
- "Can you think of any ways to apply what the preacher said to your own life?"

Discussing the sermon reinforces it to your children. It also sends the message: "I value what the preacher has to say. The sermon is important."

Second, if you know the text of the preacher's sermon in advance—for example, in churches that preach the liturgy, or in churches where the pastor announces a week in advance the text of a sermon—read that passage of Scripture with your children before the service. You may want to do this on Saturday evening. Discuss the passage a little with your children. That way, when the text is read the following day, they will be familiar with it. They will feel in sync with what is happening. They will also pay more attention to what the preacher says because they'll have some understanding about the passage.

Third, encourage your children to reiterate the sermon as best as they can in their own words.

One mother told me about how her daughter has developed a Sunday afternoon practice of "preaching to the dolls." The mother said, "Lisa told me one Sunday that since I didn't allow her to take her dolls to church, she felt they were missing out. She needed to tell them about Jesus. The next thing I knew, she had lined up all her dolls on the bed, and she was giving them her own version of the morning's sermon. She has been doing that for several months now . . . and if it isn't the dolls, it's her new puppy."

If your children know that you are going to ask them questions about the sermon or ask them to tell you what the preacher said in their own words, they will be a lot more likely to pay close attention to the sermon and to think of what it means to their lives.

As we conclude our discussion of this general issue of church conduct, let's also be aware that *our* attitude as parents toward church services can influence our children's attitude and behavior.

Don't complain about the quality of a worship service to your children. If something strikes you as inappropriate or in error, discuss it with your pastor. (Pray about your attitude and your gripe first, however!)

The story is told about a little boy who went to church with his parents, and on the way home, the father did nothing but complain. The choir was off-key; the soloist was out of sync with the pianist; the sermon was boring; the offering plate shouldn't have been so ornate; the service was too long. On and on went the criticisms. Finally, the little boy could take it no longer. He piped up from the back seat, "Well, what did you expect for a dollar, Dad— the circus?"

We get out of our church services what we put into them. What we put into them is directly related to our attitude about worship and service to the Lord.

When you negate the validity of a spiritual experience

before your children, you establish in them a spirit of criticism about the things of the Lord. You give permission for them to evaluate the church and the work of God on the basis of likes or dislikes. That is *not* the biblical criterion for discernment.

Church Quality 4:
Find a Church in Which Youths Are
Encouraged to Take an Active Role in Ministry

By ministry, of course, I'm referring here to more than lighting candles or singing in a children's choir.

Are children and teens invited to read the Scriptures?

Are children and teens invited to give a word of testimony?

Are children and teens invited to join with adults in praying for the sick or those who desire to invite Jesus Christ into their lives?

Children should be invited to minister to more than just other children. Children can minister to adults, too! Acts 10:34 assures us that God is no respecter of persons. Very often we limit the meaning of that verse to races, nationalities, or sex. God is also no respecter of a person's age. If God can use a person at age sixty, He can use a person at age six.

Of course, for children and teens to be invited to participate in these areas of ministry, the church must first provide training for them.

Church Quality 5:
Find a Church Keenly Intent
on *Training* Children to Minister to Others

Look for a church that offers your children training and experience in these areas:

• How to lead a person to Christ (in a sensitive, but direct and intentional way)

- How to prepare for, and engage in, spiritual warfare (when to recognize that an attack has been launched, how to use the Word of God to disarm the enemy, how to resist the devil so he will flee)
- How to pray for the healing of a person who is ill (in any way—physically, emotionally, mentally, spiritually)
- How to find Scriptures that pertain to specific situations, and how to share Scriptures (including how to use a concordance and how to be sensitive to the leading of the Holy Spirit)

In 1 Corinthians 1:27–31 we read,

> But God has chosen the foolish things of the world to put to shame the wise, and God has chosen the weak things of the world to put to shame the things which are mighty; and the base things of the world and the things which are despised God has chosen, and the things which are not, to bring to nothing the things that are, that no flesh should glory in His presence. But of Him you are in Christ Jesus, who became for us wisdom from God—and righteousness and sanctification and redemption—that, as it is written, "He who glories, let him glory in the LORD."

As your children are being taught to minister, they should be forewarned with this passage of Scripture. There will be those who cannot accept their ministry or who believe children aren't qualified to minister. That doesn't change the way God sees things.

Some children will see their spiritual power as being something special that they deserved, achieved, or otherwise have reason to boast about. Children who are prepared to minister should always be taught that they are equal vessels for ministry but no more than vessels. The true ministry flows *through* them to others. It is a gift from God packaged by the children. All the glory for miracles and changed lives belongs to God, and to God alone.

Church Quality 6:
Find a Church Where Members of the Church Have an Active Concern for Your Children

I have a very strong belief that if six fellow Christian adults in your church (ideally of the same sex as the child) will come to know the child's name and will seek out and express a concern for the child every Sunday before or after the worship service . . . week after week after week . . . your child will *eagerly* anticipate going to church. Church to such a child will be a place of acceptance, of friendship, of blessing, of being made to feel special in the Lord.

If each of your children doesn't have six adults as a true support group, recruit them. Form a parents' club within your church, and discuss there the importance of this bonding with the children of your congregation.

As an adult, ask yourself, Do I know six children in our church by name? If not, get to know six children. Introduce yourself to them. Find out a little about them. Take them under your wing. Befriend them.

When you see them at church, ask what they learned in Sunday school or which part of the church service they liked best. Bless them in the name of the Lord. Tell them you are gathering prayer requests, and ask if there's anything they'd like you to pray about. As your relationship with the children develops, ask them to pray about a need you are facing in your life. If a Scripture comes to mind, share it with the children as a word from the Lord with them. Give it as a word of encouragement to build up the children's faith.

Don't regard yourself as a censor. Let parents and pastors exhort. Regard yourself as an edifier—one called to build up the next generation of believers.

What About
Your Church?

Do you attend a church with these six qualities?

1. A high priority placed on children being served first
2. A desire on the part of your church leaders that your children live victorious Christian lives
3. A minister who is specifically called to *minister* to children, not entertain them
4. An active involvement of children in ministry activities
5. Training for children in *how* to minister
6. Church members, other than the pastor, who have a high level of concern for your children

If not, do what you can to foster these qualities!

Don't assume that a problem in the children's ministry of your church is the pastor's problem. Assume, instead, that it's your problem.

How many times has your pastor asked for volunteers to teach a child's Sunday school class? How many times has an announcement appeared in your church bulletin asking for adults who would be willing to sponsor youth retreats or other youth group activities?

If you want to see the approach to children changed in your church, take the initiative.

I offer these eight suggestions to you:

First, meet with other parents who may feel the same way Host an evening to discuss the situation, perhaps over a potluck supper. It may be at the church or in a home. Don't meet with a secretive agenda or with the idea that you are going to undermine the current leadership of your church. Do meet in a casual way with the intent of coming up with better solutions or alternatives.

Second, open your meeting by praying together and asking the Holy Spirit to give you His wisdom about how you might help your children to experience more of His presence Invite the Holy Spirit to be an active part of the process!

Third, give voice to your concerns Write them down in a way that all the group can see your specific concerns— using a chalkboard or big sheet of paper. Limit yourself to five or six of the foremost concerns.

Fourth, next to each concern, write the positive situation that you'd like to see take the place of the current negative one For example, you might have listed as a concern: "Children *not* included in the worship service." Next to that write what you'd like to see instead: "Children included in the worship service."

Don't allow the meeting to be primarily a pity party or a gripe session. Instead, move quickly to a consensus about what you'd like to see happen. Come up with five or six ways in which you'd like to see the children become more involved or experience more of the power and presence of God.

Fifth, discuss a way to move from each of your concerns to the ideal situation You have now moved to a discussion of ways and means. Be very practical and very precise in your suggestions. As you discuss various options . . .

• don't limit yourself in your thinking with comments such as, "That's never happened before," or "I'm not sure we'd be allowed to do that." You are better off to develop a plan and then have to modify it a bit than never to develop a plan because you are afraid it will be shot down.

• don't assume that someone else will implement the plan you design. Don't go into a planning session with the idea that "we'll get the pastor to do this" or "we'll see that the youth minister follows through on these ideas." Come up with ideas you are willing to implement yourselves.

The emphasis here is on what can you do to get from point A to point B.

Sixth, put names and dates with your plan Think in terms of who is going to do what by when. Divide the responsibilities among yourselves. Discuss whether there are other parents who might be willing to get involved in some of your ideas or plans. Identify persons on the ministerial staff you should approach with your ideas. Believe me, a pastor is much more open to an idea that is fully hatched, including names of individuals who are going to do the work, than to a vague plan that calls for the ministers to do more. Don't go to a member of the clergy staff asking the person to work harder. Let the individual know what more you and other parents would like to do.

Seventh, ask for the Lord's guidance, courage, discernment, and protection as you close the meeting with prayer Recognize that you are embarking on a bold new initiative for the Lord. In so doing, you are likely to face spiritual opposition from the enemy's camp. Pray for the spiritual protection of your children. (The last thing in the world that the devil wants to happen is for parents to get organized and to seek a greater move of the Holy Spirit among children in the church!)

Eighth, agree to intercede for your children in an ongoing way Don't plan and pray and then assume that everything will run smoothly. Make a commitment to one another to pray for your children—all of your children—by name. Get a prayer list going that ultimately includes the children of every family in your church.

As a part of your plan, make certain that every person in your group knows the names of at least six children in your church beyond those in their own family or extended family—in other words, nonrelatives. Challenge each person to take responsibility in the body of Christ for encouraging and building up each of those children. You may even want to draw names out of a hat as a "secret pal" child—one for whom you are going to pray and one you will seek out to bless. I heard of one such group of adult supporters of children that called themselves The Secret Godparents Club. What a great idea!

If all of your efforts fail in promoting a greater concern for your children's spiritual growth, I reluctantly recommend that you find a new church home.

A church that places a high priority on children will be a place your children will want to attend. I speak to many parents who say, "My children simply don't like to go to church." There may be a good reason for that. The children may not be rebelling against God or you; they may simply be bored or frustrated at what happens during their church experience. A program that truly engages the spiritual lives of children is a program that stimulates growth.

Let's Provide for Our Children
What WE Desire from Church

In conclusion . . .

Let's assume that children *do* want from a church service what we want as adults: an opportunity to experience the presence of God, to have their faith reinforced and renewed, and to discover practical ways in which the Word of God can work in their lives.

And then, let's ask how best we can provide that church experience for our children.

10

Keeping the Message
Consistent

*Though they join forces, the wicked will not go
   unpunished;
But the posterity of the righteous will be
   delivered.*

—*Proverbs 11:21*

In sharing your faith
with your children and in doing everything you know to do
to nurture your children's spiritual growth, you are taking a
stand *for* righteousness in their lives.

In taking a stand for righteousness, you must also take
a stand *against* evil.

Let me give you a brief illustration of what I mean.

Bill and Jeanne took their role as Christian parents very
seriously. They saw the spiritual nurture of their children
as their top family priority, and they adjusted their schedules and family goals accordingly. They took their children
with them to church regularly. They frequently pointed out
to their children the beauty and the working of the Lord in
the world around them. They had regular times of prayer
with their children and encouraged their children to memorize key passages of the Bible. Most important, both
showed genuine unconditional love for their children and

displayed to them a belief that their children were first-class spiritual citizens of heaven.

They liked to think of their lives and their home as marked by peace and harmony. That was their desire.

But . . .

Bill and Jeanne did not perceive that in taking such a strong stand for the "right" things in the Lord, they also needed to be taking a stand against the things of the world and the enemy that would come to entice and entrap their children.

They said yes to the things of God. But they didn't say no to the things of this world that were created for their children's demise.

What didn't they say no to?

First, they didn't say no to television. They made the assumption that many parents make about television—if it's on TV, it can't be too bad since it had to pass certain censors.

Friend, if that's what you think, too, I have some startling news for you today. The codes that regulate children's television don't put a ceiling on how many acts of violence your children will be allowed to watch in any given time period (including commercials). There are *no* codes that govern the use of occult symbols and practices being shown as a part of children's cartoons or movies. The codes limit primarily the number of minutes of commercials allowed during an hour and the use of certain words as part of dialogue.

Through an in-depth, multiyear study of children's television, my wife, Cynthia, and I came to several strong conclusions for our family:

• We do not allow our children to watch more than four to five hours of television a week, and those hours are ones that my wife, Cynthia, and I monitor like hawks. Actually, they generally aren't hours of TV but hours of video watching. For the most part, we do not allow our children to watch commercial television programming.

• We purchase videos that are edifying; we rent videos that are entertaining. We strive for a viewing experience that is 90 percent edifying and 10 percent entertaining.

• In rare cases when we allow our children to watch commercial television—such as "America's Funniest Home Videos"—we mute the commercials. We have found that our young children aren't interested in the commercials if we take the sound away. If they aren't interested in the commercials, they won't be influenced by them.

• We only rent or purchase videos or allow programming that is completely in line with our values as parents, and the values we hope to instill in our children.

Television teaches, whether we regard it as a teacher or not. It teaches children about a violent world in which crime does pay, a passionate sexual world in which there are few unwanted consequences and very few marriages and families, a world of stereotypes with very little real poverty, and a world in which problems can be presented and resolved almost instantly.

As a parent, you need to be aware that your children will *learn* spiritual values from television. They will feel the emotion of the lesson and respond to it. They will come away with subtle, even subliminal, conclusions about how people relate to one another and what the culture considers normal behavior.

In referring to television, I include the use of a television set as a monitor for viewing videotapes. Are you aware of all the movies your children watch? Or do you just send your children off to the video store, nod in agreement when they tell you that "everybody is watching this one," and then send them upstairs to watch what they want on their own VCR?

I conducted an informal survey in churches where I was

invited to speak. I asked the teens how many R-rated movies they watched and also asked them pointed questions about specific movies. I was appalled by what I heard. I calculated that teens who attended church regularly were watching nearly eighty R-rated movies a year—movies considered restricted to persons under the age of seventeen because of violence, explicit sexual images, or foul language. Eighty such movies a year! That's 160 hours, far more than the amount of spiritual experience the average teen was receiving in an entire year of attending Sunday morning church and Sunday school!

If you want your children to be good students of this world's message about life and how to live it, feed them a diet of broadcast television. If you want your children to be good students of God's message about life and how to live it, turn off broadcast TV and provide alternative messages.

Second, they didn't monitor their children's play, including their toys. Most parents I meet are more concerned with getting their children the latest thing on the market than with evaluating the true play value related to that toy or object. They want their children to be "in," and "in" usually translates "in with the world's standards."

Frankly, I'd just as soon my children be "out" of the world's clutches than be "in" with their peers.

Numerous toys are based on the violent, occult children's programs shown on television and readily available on videos and in movie theaters. Play with such toys only reinforces the values of the programs on which they have been based.

Third, they didn't monitor what their children were bringing into their home in the way of literature and music. They had a policy that their son could listen to "his" music if he kept it low and closed the door of his room. They never truly listened to the lyrics of the songs. Furthermore, both Bill and Jeanne remembered only the good old days of comic books. They hadn't seen a comic book since the days of Archie and his friends. They had no idea of the symbols and messages being read by their child . . . behind the closed door of his room with his music playing.

Fourth, they didn't keep a close watch on their children's friendships. Bill and Jeanne made an assumption that if their children were in close contact with children who lived in their upper-middle-class neighborhood or who attended their same church, all was well. That's an unwise assumption for any parent to make. Just because a family lives in your neighborhood or attends your same church does *not* mean the parents are committed to instilling and maintaining the same set of spiritual standards that you are attempting to instill in your children.

What happened to Bill and Jeanne? Their son, barely in his teens, was admitted to a mental hospital with severe depression in the wake of an attempted suicide.

Bill and Jeanne invited me to their home, asking, "What have we done wrong?" Their anguish was very real. They were filled with remorse and guilt, even though they weren't sure why their son was depressed.

The first thing I did was to pray with Bill and Jeanne that the Lord would give us His wisdom and peace in the situation. We praised God together for a good outcome for their son.

I then asked them if I could take a look in their child's room to see if there were any clues about what they might do in the future for their son's benefit.

I found a television and VCR along with several video-tapes. They were among the most violent ones I saw when I was doing the research for my book *Horror and Violence.* I found several cassette tapes of music, the lyrics of which make the blood curdle. As Bill and Jeanne and I sat in their son's room, I asked them about his friends. Bill and Jeanne quickly recognized that they didn't really know much about their son's friends, what they talked about, or what they did for fun.

I pointed out several things to Bill and Jeanne about the items that I saw in their son's room, and it was as if a light had been turned on. Jeanne kept saying, "I had no idea." Please recognize that I didn't share with them to bring condemnation on them; I spoke from the perspective of "what we can do from here on." After our talk, we prayed together again—right there in the boy's room. We filled that bedroom with praise. We entered into deep intercession for their son, even as we picked up various objects and removed them from the room, some into the trash, some into the closet of the family room. And then, we mapped out a plan for what Bill and Jeanne might do once their son returned home.

What had happened in the family's life?

Their child had received very mixed signals. In a way, it's as if their son had been listening to music with a stereo headset. On one channel, through one ear piece, he was hearing praises to God. He was experiencing the power and presence of the Lord and the unlimited, unconditional love of his parents.

On the other channel, however, through the other ear piece, he was hearing the wail of the world. He was encountering violence, evil, and horror in megadoses.

The two channels didn't mesh, and the result was a tremendously discordant set of messages playing loudly in his mind. He was literally being ripped apart on the inside in a battle for his very soul.

The front door of his life had been opened up to the glory of God. The back door of his life, however, had not been closed to evil.

Shutting the
Door on Evil

What must a parent do in shutting the door on evil?

First, recognize that you must say no to evil's presence in a child's life from the time the child is born Don't expect to clean out your closet or refrigerator or bookcase when a child begins to walk, talk, or explore. Do it before your child is born.

Children see and feel long before they understand.

Second, don't allow television to be your children's primary teacher Closely monitor any program that your children watch. Look for signs of violence, sexual jokes or overtones, or occult symbols. If you don't know what those symbols might be, do some research.

Not only should you watch for quality of programming, but you need to put a ceiling on the quantity of television you will allow your children to consume. Active play is always more beneficial to them than passive viewing.

If your children see something of which you don't approve—perhaps in the home of a friend—discuss the program with them. Express your concerns. Mediate the impact that program might have on your children's lives.

Television has become such a mainstay in so many of our homes, it's difficult for some parents to think of what their children might do if they weren't watching TV. If you need suggestions in this area, I recommend these two practical little books:

- *52 of the Best Toys and Games for Your Child*
- *52 Things for Your Kids to Do Instead of Watching TV*

Third, choose toys, games, and other play activities with care Your children learn through play. It's how they make sense of the world. By monitoring the things that they play with, and the activities in which they engage, you can point them away from spiritual danger even as you promote spiritual growth.

As general guidelines, I offer these suggestions:

• *Point your children toward games and toys that require them to make up the story line, create characterizations, and envision environments as they play.* This is an active process that engages their mental, emotional, and physical energies. I do *not* recommend toys related to movies, television programs, or video games. These toys promote what I call prescribed play. Children tend to imitate with the toy what they have seen the character do in the media program rather than make up their own plots. As such, they are mimicking behavior rather than using their creativity. If children tell you, "This is what this toy does," be wary of it. As a parent, two of the best questions you can ask about a toy or game are: What will my children do *with* it? What will they learn from playing with this item?

• *Develop a love of reading in your children by reading to them and with them.* Go to the library periodically with them. Help your children choose books that are challenging, uplifting, and interesting.

• *Only buy toys for your children that are high in play value—durable toys and activities that can be used through many years and provide hours of involvement.* Building sets, crayons and other art supplies, dolls, parlor games, and outdoor play items (such as bicycles, jump ropes, sidewalk chalk) are just a few examples of items that your children will return to again and again.

Fourth, guard your home against the invasion of ungodly messages It is your prerogative as a parent to monitor what happens in your home, even what is played, read, or seen in your children's rooms. I'm all for showing respect for your children's privacy and desire to be alone, but I am

100 percent against allowing them to consume evil privately in the confines of a room with a closed door.

I suggest a policy of "closed door is okay, locked door is not." Let your children know that you have the right to enter their rooms at any time. As a general rule, keep the doors of their rooms open to the rest of the house. They are part of a family; their rooms are part of the family home.

If you find materials in their rooms or possession—such as comic books, books, magazines, music, or posters—of which you don't approve, discuss your feelings with them. Be able to express why you disapprove of the item and why you must insist that it not be in your home.

Should your children want to bring in a baby boa constrictor as a pet, you as a parent would probably insist that the reptile be removed at once. Regard evil messages with the same concern. Insist that the material be removed, and explain why. Your children's spiritual future may be at stake. Let them know that you are making this decision and insisting upon this action because you love them too much to see them enticed by evil.

This same policy applies to any item that is chemically inappropriate for your children: alcohol, nicotine products, drugs. Insist immediately that the items be removed. Explore how your children came to have possession of such items and why they felt a need for them.

I am always shocked to find Christian parents who keep alcohol, nicotine products, and other addictive chemicals in their homes for their own adult use. In so many cases, these parents will state with strong conviction that they don't want their children to use these products or become addicted to them. Still, they continue to use them, and in so doing, they model a behavior of acceptance to their children. Such parents are victims of the "do what I say, not what I do" syndrome. Face the facts. Children will do what you do. They will always look for what you do to line up with what you say. If you are addicted to a product that you don't want your children to become addicted to, get help . . . starting today.

Fifth, monitor your children's friendships I'm not suggesting that you spy on your children, that you choose all of their friends for them, or that you insist on being with your children and their friends at all times. Not only would you be manipulating and suffocating your children, you would be greatly limiting their ability to make decisions.

I do suggest that you get to know their friends. Take time to talk to them. Find out what they like and don't like. Listen to them. You can learn a lot over a bowl of popcorn, in an afternoon of fishing, or in a couple hours of experimenting with hairstyles and giving free "Mom manicures."

Also get to know the parents of your children's friends. Talk over ways in which you might take a mutual stand against peer pressure.

Watch the way in which your children play with friends. How do they communicate with them?

Is the play always violent? Does one child always seem to get her way? Is one child possessive or obsessive about the relationship? Does one child dominate a conversation?

What activities do your children and their friends enjoy?

Do you notice any changes in your children's behavior after being with certain children? Do they use language of which you don't approve? Do they show signs of being angry or frustrated? Are they more rebellious against you? Do they have more nightmares or increased incidents of bed-wetting? If so, find new friends for your children.

Sixth, know where your children are when they aren't at home, school, or church Insist that your children tell you the truth about where they are going, who they are going with, and what they anticipate they will be doing. Be cautious about letting your children go home with friends when the friends' parents aren't there.

Don't interrogate your children about time spent away from you. Do express interest. Listen for what your children may drop as hints in a conversation. Children who have open and genuine communication with a parent will generally express their discomfort or concern about activities they suspect may not be good, although that expression may be a bit veiled.

For example, your child may say, "Wow, that was some party." Don't assume that your child is telling you he had a great time. He may be telling you that things were happening at the party that he didn't understand or didn't know how to evaluate. Ask simply, "What happened?" or "Did you have a good time?" Listen closely to the answer.

I believe you are wise when you have a general policy regarding your children:

Trust your children.
Never trust the enemy of your children's souls.

Sometimes the enemy can work through children's friendships. Be alert to that possibility.

Bear in mind, too, that you have both the authority and the responsibility for the places your children go and the activities you allow your children to experience. You *do* have the right to say, "No, you may not go."

In many cases, children are relieved when a parent says, "No, you may not see that show," or "No, that isn't something I want you to experience."

At times, you may want to give an explanation to your children about why you are making that decision. At other times, you may make a decision strictly on the basis of your parental instincts. Let them know you are making a decision that you feel is for the best, and they simply will have to trust you with that. If you're wrong, you're sorry. If you're right, they'll be exceedingly glad later in life. Don't give in to whining, pleading, or cajoling.

The best defense, of course, is usually a good offense. Suggest a better alternative to your children. Plan activities. Keep them involved in good things: attending good events, going fun places, and having good experiences. They won't miss the bad times they know nothing about.

Seventh, refuse to allow profanity in your home or the taking of the Lord's name in vain Children experiment with language. Most parents don't realize that children learn to think based on the words they know. Our thought process as human beings is intricately intertwined with our vocabulary. We cannot think beyond the concepts we know; everything else is intuition or sensory. When children are allowed to use profanity or to use the name of the Lord lightly or disrespectfully, a spirit of vulgarity and disrespect takes root in the children's spirits.

You have the authority to insist that the words spoken in your home are pure and innocent before the Lord. Don't allow your children to develop a home vocabulary and a church vocabulary. You'll instill in them a mind-set that separates the work of the Lord from the totality of their lives. The very opposite is your goal as a Christian parent.

Eighth, never laugh at or ignore your children's sin I once overheard a parent say during a child's temper tantrum, "Isn't she cute when she's angry?" I nearly swallowed my teeth.

Children are never cute or funny when they display disobedient behavior or an attitude that is rooted in hatred, anger, or lust. Refuse to tolerate or applaud such behavior.

Gardens Need Weeding

One of the best ways I know to approach the training of children to love and serve the Lord is to see them as tender young vines in the Lord's vineyard. They need to have all of the good provision necessary for growth—the Sonshine of the Lord Jesus, the water of the Holy Spirit, the nutrients from the life-sustaining soil of God's Word, the training of their lives along the ethical and moral vines ordered by the Lord.

Vines also need pruning. Vineyards need weeding.

A good environment must be established for your children as a place to grow and develop spiritually. That environment must also be hedged off from evil, and any outcropping of evil within your home must be eliminated as quickly as it is recognized.

If you have let some things go in your home—things that the Holy Spirit is convicting you about—today is a day of action for you. There's still something you can do. Begin taking steps today to release the enemy's grip on your home and to put in place new policies and procedures to make your home a "no evil" zone.

Let your children know what you are doing and why. Express to them your deep sorrow for not having recognized previously the need to stand more strongly against evil. Enlist their help in the process.

Affirm always that in standing against evil, you are keeping at bay the very dogs that would try to rip your children's souls apart. You are removing the weeds that, if left to grow wild, will overtake the good fruit from your garden. You are stamping out pests before they multiply out of control and create constant confusion and unrest in your home. Whatever visual image you choose, let your children know that the action you are taking is one that you believe in strongly for the eternal benefit of all your souls.

If it isn't a part of heaven—something pleasing and beneficial that you would like to have in your life for all eternity—it shouldn't be a part of your home on earth.

Gathering Allies
for Your Purposes

In many ways, you as a Christian parent are in a battle against the world for your children. Every warring nation knows the importance of strongly defended borders. Beyond that first line of defense, however, you need an offense. And an offense generally includes allies.

In seeking allies, don't let yourself be limited to your relatives or to your church body for help in training your children. Find others who can support and reinforce the values and behaviors that you are attempting to instill in your children.

Consider a Christian School for Your Children

Your children will be in school for more waking hours than they will be in your presence in the home (at least from the time they are five years old until after high school) and for at least nine months of the year. A Christian school—with God-fearing, Bible-believing, Jesus-exalting, Spirit-led teachers and principals—is one way of surrounding yourself with others who share a commitment to the value system that you are attempting to instill in your children.

Choose the school with care. Not all Christian schools are created equal. Find one using a curriculum that you can support wholeheartedly. Talk to the teachers and principal. Meet some of the other parents and get their impressions of the quality and nature of education their children are receiving. Observe a classroom in action.

If you do enroll your children in a Christian school, take an active part as a parent. Attend parent-teacher conferences. Volunteer, if you are able, to help out periodically as a teacher's aide or room parent. Experience your children's education in process. The closer the harmony between what you are instilling in them at home and what is being taught to them at school, the better the results.

What if no Christian school is available to you, or you are unable to afford a Christian school? Then get to know the teachers at your local public school. Many public school teachers are Christians. Seek out those professionals, and request the placement of your children in their classes. The teachers may not be able to discuss the Bible or religious values in the classroom, but they will display personal values that are likely to be closer to your own than those of teachers who claim to be agnostics, atheists, or cult members.

Develop and Associate with Friends who Share Your Values and Have Children the Ages of Your Own

They may be friends from church. They may be Christian friends in your neighborhood who attend a variety of churches. Spend time with these friends. Cultivate more than just casual friendships. Go on outings and picnics and retreats together. Let your children see firsthand that what they are being taught at home is *also* being taught in the homes of their friends.

Having such a circle of friends does three great things for your children:

1. *It provides them with peers who are under similar authority before the Lord.* All youngsters experience peer pressure. It helps if peers are being required to live under the same value system as your children. Peer-pressure problems arise primarily when children associate with a group that is being raised under a value system different from the one in your home. These peers can become wonderful lifelong friends. They also provide a ready-made alternative group with whom your children might associate should school friends pursue activities that go against the value system you are attempting to establish in their lives. For example, if all the children in your children's school

are going to a Halloween party, the children in your group of Christian friends may get together for an alternative party that reflects Christ-honoring values rather than vestiges of evil Druid practices.

2. *It gives your children other adults with whom they might discuss their problems or ideas.* Children at some point in growing up need to see and hear what Christian adults, other than parents, think about life. If your children have a problem that they don't feel they can discuss with you, it's better to have them take that problem to a Christian friend of yours than to take it to non-Christian peers or to sublimate it where it will only fester and grow larger.

3. *It provides an opportunity for your children to witness a variety of family structures and methods of communicating, even within the body of Christ.* Christian Family A may be far more structured and formal than Christian Family B. One family may have a different cultural background. Yet another family may have a gifted child or a disabled child. Each family, of course, will have its own schedules and activities and affiliations and unique call of ministry. Still, all can love and serve the Lord Jesus. Your children will benefit from seeing that there is more than one way to live out Christian values.

Seek Christian Youth Activities for Your Children

It may be a youth group at church. It may be a Scout group with a Christian troop leader. It may be a swim club or a softball team with a Christian coach.

Choose Professionals who Are Christians

I would never advocate going to second-best professionals just because they claim Jesus as Lord, but I do have a strong belief that many top-notch Christians are working in virtually all professions, and that we parents are wise to seek out these professionals for our children. A Christian dentist or physician is more likely to see your children as whole persons and to relate to them as young warriors of the faith. Find a Christian art, ballet, or music teacher for your children. All instruction is couched in some type of value structure; the closer that value system is to your own, the more likely your children's values will be reinforced even as they learn new skills.

Make Christ-Honoring Media Materials Available

You may not like the beat of your children's music. In fact, you probably won't like it any more than your parents liked the music you enjoyed as a child or teen. But you can exert influence over the lyrics of the songs to which your children listen.

A number of fiction and nonfiction books are on the market that reflect Christian values to teens. *Campus Life* magazine is a long-standing mainstay for the Christian teenager.

Make yourself aware of the videos and films that have values with which you can agree as a Christian. I heartily recommend to all parents this publication edited by John H. Evans:

Family Video Guide
Movie Morality Ministries, Inc.
1309 Seminole Drive
Richardson, TX 75080-3736

Words of Caution

Many parents assume that any person who claims the title of Christian lives out the spiritual life in the same way they do. The same holds true for their opinion of materials labeled Christian. Don't be naive in this area. The fact is that many people who call themselves Christian won't express their faith or live out their Christian beliefs in keeping with the way you do.

Ask questions of those to whom you entrust your children. Find out exactly what they believe about God's Word,

Jesus Christ, and your children's position in the kingdom of God.

Also listen closely to what your children say about the materials and associations you have provided to them as beyond-the-home-and-church resources. Ask them questions about what they are learning from particular persons, courses, or books.

Keep in mind that you as a parent *always* have the primary responsibility for your children's welfare and development, and that you are the one who gives other adults the authority they have over your children. If you suspect that any person is abusing that authority or is attempting to undermine the values and Christian principles that you are attempting to develop in your children, remove your children from that person's presence—regardless of a Christian label.

And finally, watch for fruit in your children's lives as the result of their association with other Christians. Encourage the development of the good traits you see emerging. Be on the alert for behaviors that are not in line with those you have encouraged in your home.

Maintain close communication with other persons—teachers, coaches, youth leaders—to whom you entrust your children. Ask their opinion on your children's spiritual growth. You can benefit greatly from their insights, and you may also be blessed to hear reports of your children's witness about which you would otherwise be unaware.

Your Greatest Ally
Is the Lord Himself

Your greatest ally in training your children, of course, is the Lord Himself. Solicit His help . . . daily!

You may want to post these words from Psalm 127 where you can read them often:

Unless the LORD builds the house,
They labor in vain who build it;
Unless the LORD guards the city,
The watchman stays awake in vain.
It is vain for you to rise up early,
To sit up late,
To eat the bread of sorrows;
For so He gives His beloved sleep.
Behold, children are a heritage from the LORD,
The fruit of the womb is a reward.
Like arrows in the hand of a warrior,
So are the children of one's youth.
Happy is the man who has his quiver full of them;
They shall not be ashamed,
But shall speak with their enemies in the gate.

11

Facing Your Family's Future with Hope

Now all Judah, with their little ones, their wives, and their children, stood before the LORD.
—2 Chronicles 20:13

The day will come when you and your children will stand before the Lord.

If that thought sends a fear of judgment coursing through your spirit rather than an excitement about reward, this chapter is for you.

A recurring theme throughout the Scriptures is this: We get what we believe for. Seeing isn't believing to the Christian. Believing results in seeing: "Now faith is the substance of things hoped for, the evidence of things not seen" (Heb. 11:1).

What are you believing for in the lives of your children —indeed, in the life of every member of your family?

Ask the Lord to Give You a Revelation for Your Family

Ask the Lord to give you a new revelation of who He is . . . who your children are . . . and who your family can be in Him.

Every family has a purpose for being on this earth. We often tend to think of individuals having a reason for being. What is true for the individual is also true for a family. God is the One who puts individuals together into families. The family was His idea.

Ask the Lord to show you what your purpose is as a family on the earth. You should certainly pray for this revelation to come to both you and your spouse. It isn't enough for a husband alone or a wife alone to experience this revelation. The Lord always confirms His word out of the mouth of "two or three witnesses." Look for that to hold true, also, as He reveals your family's purpose to you.

You may want to invite your children to participate in this process with you. You may want to come together humbly before the Lord on a weekend retreat as a family. As you read the Scriptures together and individually, and pray together as a family and individually, and then meditate on God's Word and listen for God's voice . . . ask the Lord to show you who He desires for you to be on this earth.

Every Christian family bears these purposes in common:

• *To be a witness to your neighborhood and surrounding community that you love and serve the Lord.* Your neighbors need to know that Jesus is the Lord of your home. They need to know that they have the freedom to meet Jesus there at any time they desire to come to know Him.

• *To be a fountain of praise to the Lord on the earth.* We are called as God's people, clustered into families, to be a habitation for God's presence. And wherever God's presence is, there must surely be praise. The psalmist declared, "You are holy, enthroned in the praises of [Your chosen people]" (Ps. 22:3).

• *To be a refuge apart from this world.* Your home is to be a haven of rest—a place of peace—where evil has no toehold and no influence.

• *To be a place of mutual support and encouragement for each member of the family.* We are not called to walk our path through this world by ourselves. We are called to be the body of Christ to one another—to help others along the way, to encourage and to edify, to bless and to exhort, to lift up and to heal. We are especially called to do this in the context of family love. The home is to be a place of nurture for each member of the family.

• *To be a place where the law of the Lord is put into effect and lived out and, thereby, made manifest on this earth.* Your home is to be something of a colonial outpost of heaven on this earth; it is intended to operate according to the principles and commandments of heaven with full allegiance to heaven. Your home is the primary place for you to learn and to put into practice the teachings of God's Word.

• *To pray together as a family in intercession for the needs of your greater family, your church, your city, your nation, and the world.*

• *To stand together as a family in heaven one day, and to hear the Lord say, "Well done, good and faithful servants."*

The nightmare of nightmares is to arrive in heaven without a member of your family. The horror of horrors is for family members to fail one another as Christian brothers and sisters.

As you pray and seek God's revelation about your family, consider these basic principles, and then ask the Lord to quicken to each one of you specific ways in which these principles can be put into effect.

Should you perhaps host a neighborhood barbecue and make that an opportunity to share your faith with your neighbors? Should you make a special point of inviting your neighbors to go with you to church? What other things can you do to give witness to the Lord Jesus to your neighbors?

What adjustments might be made in your home to establish greater peace and more praise? Should some family activities be curtailed or eliminated? Should some new family policies or procedures be implemented? In what new ways might your family bond together spiritually?

You may want to consider establishing

• a new commitment to prayer as a family.

• a new commitment to attending Wednesday evening church services as a family.

• a family prayer list posted in a place where it is readily seen by all family members.

• a read-through-the-Bible plan that every member of the family can follow, with periodic dinner table conversations about what you have been reading.

Each family will come up with adjustments to the spiritual life that are unique to the family situation. In virtually all cases, these new adjustments will be a challenge— usually for every member of the family.

To establish new habits as a family, old habits may need to be discarded. To reset priorities, schedules may need to be adjusted. Some compromises in household chores may need to be made. Schedule changes and changes of habit are tough to make. Recognize at the outset that it may be difficult to cast away some of the things that keep the family from growing in the Lord. Agree to help one another in the process. Seal that agreement in prayer together.

Consider, too, new ways in which members of your family might support one another more effectively and powerfully. What areas of family communication need to be opened up? What family ties need to be strengthened or renewed?

Gain a Vision for Lost Souls

As you seek God's revelation for your family, ask Him to give your family a vision for lost souls. That vision of the world will no doubt result in a deep desire to see the gospel taken into areas where it has never been heard, to see souls saved, and to see deliverance of those in spiritual bondage.

One of the greatest callings God can ever place on a family is to call that family to pray and intercede for the lost of this world.

You may want to use a map of your city, a listing of your city officials, or even a local phone book to guide your prayer as a family for the people of your city.

You may want to pray through the names of the families in your local church directory.

You may want to use a map of your state or your nation or a globe or world map as a visual aid to guide your prayer.

Here are some suggestions about what to pray for:

• Pray that the leaders of that city, state, or nation will establish peace so that the gospel can go forward, that missionaries and evangelists will be allowed to share their message of the gospel freely, and that gospel literature will be readily available and be allowed to be distributed throughout that area.

• Pray that the children of that city, state, or nation will be protected from harm and that someone will reach them with the good news that God loves them.

• Pray that new churches will be established, led by men and women who truly love the Lord and who will be faithful ministers of God's Word.

• Pray for the safety of Christians who live in that area. Pray that they will be made ever more bold in their witness. Pray for the missionaries or Christian evangelists who may be at work in that area, that their work will be effective and they personally will be kept in safety and health.

• Pray that innovative ways of sharing the good news will be developed to reach the people who live in that area —in a language they can understand and a method they can readily embrace as part of their culture.

The family that sees its call, or certainly a part of its call, as a call to intercede for the lost souls of this world is a family that has a strong focus for its prayer life. Through such prayer, children can develop a keen awareness of the work of the Lord in the world and the dire effects of living in a place where the gospel isn't heard or among people who don't honor and serve the Lord.

You and your spouse can begin times of intercession for the lost from the day each child is born. Let your children grow up hearing you pray for lost souls in Gambia, Afghanistan, Korea, or Chile. Soon they will be joining with you. Soon they will be spinning the globe on their own, asking the Holy Spirit to move in nations and in cities to bring lost souls to Himself. Children raised with this orientation toward prayer will no doubt be much more interested in studying geography, history, and languages. They'll be involved in the world—not only as active political citizens but as spiritual leaven.

You may find that your family's prayer focus includes prayer for the salvation of the leaders of certain nations. You may even want to write a family letter to those leaders to let them know that you are praying for them.

You may find that your family develops an interest in taking a short-term mission trip some summer to one of the nations for which you have prayed a great deal in the past.

You may find that your family begins to correspond with missionaries or believers in a faraway place.

You may find that your family takes on a project to help

build a church or Christian school or hospital in a faraway place.

The gospel was always intended to start at home and to work at home, but it was never intended to stay at home.

Look for God's Unique Call on Your Family

Beyond the general and foundational purposes for your family as intercessors, worshipers, and witnesses on this earth, look for the Lord also to give you a mission as a family that may be unique to your family. Your family has a unique set of combined talents, gifts, interests, and abilities. Just as God uses individuals in unique ways, so, too, He uses a family. Ask God to reveal to you His special call for what you can do to further His kingdom on this earth.

God may lead you to support a particular missionary or evangelist in a special way. That wonderful call has been placed on many families in our nation. I know of several families that support evangelists as their special call from God. They faithfully pray for their representative daily and support him regularly. As a family, they have special projects for saving money or raising additional funds to send for special projects. For every family that God calls to go on the road or overseas with the gospel, He also calls dozens of others to rally in support of that family.

God may call you as a family to rent a billboard in your community for a month to proclaim the gospel message or to give a message of thanksgiving and praise to the Lord. One family did that in honor of a son who was brought home safely from a dangerous situation. The billboard read, "We thank the Lord Jesus Christ for the safe return of our son from Nicaragua, and thank you for your prayers on his behalf."

God may call you to be one of the faithful families that cares for the people who come to your church's door in search of assistance.

God may call you as a family to provide something tangible for your church. One family felt called to fully outfit the nursery in their church with new cribs. The entire family worked at this goal—going out together on Saturdays as a yard crew to mow lawns. They used all of their proceeds to fund their project. They didn't see it as a burden. They saw it as fulfilling a call from the Lord specifically to their family, and they experienced great joy in accomplishing this goal the Lord had set before them.

Don't limit what the Lord might call you to do or to be for Him. Don't seek His revelation with an "I'm certain God would never ask us to do that" attitude. Recognize at the outset that if God calls you to undertake a specific task, He will equip you for accomplishing that task both materially and spiritually, and He will give you joy as you step out in faith to do what He calls you to do.

A Vision About and for Your Family Provides a Spiritual Focus

The Scriptures tell us that the people of God perish when they have no prophetic vision about who they are or where they are going. Proverbs 29:18 literally says, "Where there is no revelation, the people cast off restraint; but happy is he who keeps the law."

Without a vision for your family—who you are called to be by the Lord, and what you are called to do on this earth to extend His kingdom—it will be difficult for your family to stay focused on spiritual growth and outreach as your top family priority. You will become scattered in your purpose. As you do, you no doubt will find that various diversions will creep into your family schedule and into your family's realm of experience. These diversions may come in the form of books, magazines, music, videos, or other media messages that are allowed in your home . . . new people you invite to share the peace of your home . . . new activities that you allow to be implemented in your home . . . or new events that you allow to be scheduled in place of spiritual activities you enjoyed as a family in the past. You know they are diversions if they keep you from experiencing the fullness of God's best for your family.

Let me be very practical about this. I recently heard of a family—actually, the family of a prominent leader in his local church—that missed church and Sunday school for three Sundays in a row. The pastor finally called the father of the family and asked if anything was wrong. The man didn't register the least bit of chagrin as he responded, "No, nothing's wrong, pastor. Our son's soccer team just had games on those Sunday mornings."

Nothing was wrong? In my opinion, something was very wrong. When soccer games can take the place of Sunday morning worship together as a family, which was the family's only scheduled weekly spiritual activity *as a family*, there's definitely a lack of spiritual focus in that family— no matter what church boards the father may be elected to serve on. I firmly believe that if the family had experienced a true revelation from the Lord about who they are to be as a family, and what they are called by the Lord to do for Him on this earth, they would know precisely where they need to be on Sunday mornings.

Which brings us to another important point . . .

Ask the Lord to Show You His Purpose and Role for Your Family as Part of Your Local Church

When we truly make Jesus the Lord of our local church— and by that I mean, when we truly consult Him as a church body and ask for His direction and wisdom in all of the ways our church is to organize itself, operate, build itself up spiritually, and reach out to others—we can trust the Lord to fit us together. The metaphor of a building "jointly fitted together" is one that the apostle Paul uses frequently in his letters to the early church. It's a metaphor worth reconsidering today. What part of your local church are you?

Elsewhere in the Scriptures we read that the godly are to be pillars in the house of the Lord. What a wonderful picture that evokes!

In both examples, the truth we see is that we—as individuals *and* as families—have a role to play in our local church body. We are to support our church with our attendance, our gifts, and our service.

The ways in which we render that service should be a matter of family prayer and commitment, children included.

Make a commitment to have your children in Sunday school every week—not just on an as-you-feel-like-it or if-the-weather-is-good basis.

Make a commitment to attend church regularly.

Make a commitment to give regularly.

Make a commitment to serve others in your church body in some way.

A pastor shared with me the story of one family in his congregation that had a practice for years of taking produce from their garden to church in the back of their station wagon every Sunday from late spring to fall. They prepared a special box of fresh vegetables and fruits for each pastor, and then they invited other church members to share in their abundance as they desired. This rural family attended church in a city, and in their congregation, many families were barely making ends meet financially. A little sack of fresh vegetables and fruits was a great blessing to them. The pastor told me that on one Sunday, he watched the family give away fifty small sacks of produce. Talk about serving your brothers and sisters in Christ!

Recognize that the commitment of one family member to a position of leadership or service is actually a commitment of the entire family. For example, a Sunday school teacher cannot teach adequately without all other members of the family giving the person the time and quiet to prepare lessons. A person cannot prepare and deliver a meal for someone who is newly home from a hospital stay without cooperation from other family members. Consider your family before you say yes to a church request for your services. Make certain that you have the full support of your family for the job, and that the members realize they will share in your heavenly reward for the task well done.

Look for the Possibility of the Lord Leading You from One Mission Purpose to Another

Finally, recognize that God may lead your family from one special call to another. As you accomplish one task that the Lord puts before you to do, look for a new one from Him. Don't choose to rest on your laurels as a family. Continually seek the Lord's guidance about what more He may desire for you or from you.

The same holds true for some family practices. One family felt called by God to keep Saturday as a day of rest before Him—a true sabbath in which very little work was done. Family members used the day as a time to reflect, renew, relax, and refresh themselves in the Lord and in the presence of other family members. On some Saturdays they rode bicycles and had picnics in the parks of their city. Some Saturdays they just curled up in front of the family fireplace and read books or played games together. The Lord called this family to keep this practice in effect for several years, and then He called them to use Saturdays as a time of intense family outreach to their community. The years of rest and relaxation together had truly caused a deep bonding of the family members to one another so that when the Lord called them to begin giving in a way that required a great deal of family effort and coordination, they were already forged into a solid working unit with high morale and good communication.

Another family experienced the Lord's leading in a very

different way. The Lord led them as a family to be intensely involved with a Scouting program at their church. They led an average of one overnight campout a month with various members of their church youth group for several years. The events took a great deal of family planning, sacrifice, and a high degree of commitment on the part of each family member.

And then the day came when the Lord led them in a new direction—a release from the intense obligation. Each member of the family felt great freedom to find a new individual area of service in the church. One taught Sunday school. Another began working in the church nursery. Yet another ladled out soup to the homeless who came to the church's back door on Sunday mornings. The family was no less involved in the church, but on an individual basis rather than as a family.

Did this new direction subtract from their feelings of togetherness? On the contrary. They met purposefully once a week as a family to pray for one another and to support one another in their new avenues of ministry. They took time to share openly with one another their personal challenges and their needs. At times, they substituted for one another. One type of service simply became another type of service.

At other times, the Lord may call you into a position of service that truly becomes a lifelong call. I recently met a couple who had experienced this. The mother of the family started teaching Sunday school to toddlers (two-year-olds, to be exact) when her own firstborn child reached that age. She felt a special anointing from the Lord for the task and truly looked forward to sharing the good news with the group of little ones she met in the basement of the church each week. Believe me, a person who feels anointed and called to teach two-year-olds is a special person in my eyes!

This woman has been teaching two-year-olds for the

past thirty-eight years. She's still at it. She still feels called and anointed for the job. She's taught an entire generation of children in that church, many of whom have now brought *their* children to the door of her Sunday school class.

During the Sunday school hour, her husband goes with a country-western-style group from the church to sing gospel songs at the city jail just a few blocks from their downtown church building. One of the men in the group generally shares a word of personal testimony or a passage of Scripture. They are there about a half hour. Not only do they sing and share with the prisoners, but they pray with them. He, too, has been doing this for thirty-eight years. He's still at it, many guitar strings and a couple of guitars later.

What about their sons? When the boys were young, Dad and the boys fixed Sunday morning breakfasts so Mom could finish preparing the Sunday school lesson for her class. Then as the boys married and had families of their own, they joined their dad in going to the local jail on Sunday mornings. One of the young men said, "What else *would* I do at ten o'clock on a Sunday morning?"

The common thread in each of these family examples is this: They viewed their ministry together *as a family.* As they served the Lord together, they grew together, both as a natural family and as a spiritual unit.

What is *your* family ministry today? Can you identify it? Or are you going your separate ways, doing what each chooses to do?

If you don't have a family ministry or a vision for your family, ask the Lord to give you one today. I feel 100 percent confident that He will.

Ask the Lord to Give Your Children a Revelation About Their Lives

One of the most common questions that we adults ask children is, "What do you want to be when you grow up?"

Perhaps as Christian parents and adults, we need to ask our younger brothers and sisters in the Lord, "What is God calling you to be when you grow up?"

Every profession can be a profession used by the Lord. There's never a time when children are too young to have that idea conveyed to them.

Ask God to give your children a vision for their lives.

Joseph was only seventeen years old when God gave him a dream of his destiny. (See Gen. 37.)

Jesus knew at the age of twelve that He was to be about His Father's business. (See Luke 2.)

Mary was probably just a teenager when the angel Gabriel visited her and announced that she had been chosen by God to be the mother of the Messiah. (See Luke 1:26–38.) ·

Jeremiah was but a child when the Lord called him to be a prophet to a nation. (See Jer. 1:4–8.)

Let your children know that you expect them to have and to follow the vision for their lives as the Lord gives it. The story of David and Solomon provides us with clear evidence that a parent's vision doesn't translate to a child. David envisioned building a great temple for God. The Lord told him that he would not be allowed to build it, but that his son would. Solomon began his reign as king with David's vision in his heart. However, as soon as he had completed the construction and the dedication of the temple, Solomon began to "love many foreign women" who enticed him to serve their gods. (See 1 Kings 11:1–11.) Solomon lacked a vision from God for his own life.

God sees your children as Christian soldiers in the making. He sees them as people who will do mighty exploits for and in the name of the Lord.

Our job is not only to see our children born again but to see them grow up into the fullness of Christ. Help your children envision that fullness without specifying roles for them. Let the Lord supply the details, the plan, and the means to your children.

A vision for the future gives hope.

With hope comes joy.

Become a Fountain of Joy Before Your Children

Let your children know that your faith in the Lord gives you joy. Be free to laugh with them about life, human foibles, and even those things in church that strike you as humorous. Don't instill in your children an impression that God never smiles. His foremost command to us is to "fear not, rejoice!" Surely, joy is something the Lord must feel about and for us if it's something He desires us to feel about and for Him.

Let your children know that you are grateful for His Word. Express thanksgiving for the Bible. It's so easy to say as you read a Bible story, "I'm so glad God gave us His Word so we can know how to use it in our lives."

Let your children know that you have a sense of wonder about the Lord. Be amazed at who God is, how He works, and what God is doing in the world. Stand in awe at His creation. Share with them the joy you feel in being part of God's world.

Let your children know how important your family is to you as a parent—and how critically important each child is to the family. Your children will intuitively pick this up through your comments about your family to others, through how much time you spend with your family, and through the choices you make in which family is revealed to be a priority. Don't overlook the obvious, however. *Tell* your children how important they are to the family and how important the family is to you. Tell them what joy they give you.

The same principle extends to the church. Let your children know how important your church family is to you, and how much you value the time spent at church and in Christian fellowship.

Let your children know that you have enthusiasm for His church. Express high hopes for the future of the body of Christ. Speak well of Christian leaders. Show respect always for your pastor (or pastors).

If You Don't Feel Joy—
Ask God to Renew Joy within You!

Are you feeling low on joy today because you feel you have already "blown it" with your children? Perhaps they are already teenagers or older, or you may feel that you have lost your children in some way through divorce or separation.

Take heart! Throughout the Scriptures we see evidence again and again that God is capable of working a miracle regardless of circumstances. No situation is ever too late or too bad for God.

If you haven't prayed with diligence for your children in the past, begin to intercede for them today. Cry out to God for their souls. Ask God for wisdom about how you might relate to your children the faith that you have, in a way that they will perceive as genuine and sincere.

If you haven't shared with your children the importance of your relationship with the Lord Jesus Christ, make an appointment with them to do so. Find a time. Find a suitable place.

You may need to apologize to your children or ask their forgiveness before they will be able to hear what you have to say. Ask the Lord to help you do that. It's never easy to admit that you have made a mistake, much less admit that you have made a mistake as a parent, much less admit that to your own children. Still, for your children truly to hear what you have to say, that step may be critical for you to take.

Let your children know that you have made a new commitment to the Lord to pray for them. Share with them the deep desire of your heart *not* to live in eternity without them. Express your love for your children, and let them know that *you* know that your love comes from the heavenly Father, who loves you all.

As long as children live under your roof and you have some responsibility for them, you also have authority over them and what takes place in your home. Even if your children are teens, it's not too late for you to make adjustments in your family schedule to include regular church attendance, family prayer, or involvement in ministry outreach.

The enemy may come to you repeatedly and tempt you, saying, "You've lost your children." Don't buy into that lie! Stand firm and say, "No. I refuse to believe that. I'm going to believe God for a spiritual miracle in the life of every member of my family. I stand as the parent of these children and declare, 'My children will love and serve the Lord. They will come to know Him in a life-changing, eternally living way!'"

Ask the Lord to give you new faith to believe for your children. Ask the Lord to take away any fear that wells up within you. Above all, ask the Lord to forgive you for your mistakes of the past, to give you courage for the future, and to free you from living under any condemnation the enemy may try to place on you.

All parents, including Christian parents, make mistakes. Christian conversion is not a vaccine against error. Desiring to follow and serve the Lord doesn't ensure that you won't make a bad judgment call or strike out occasionally. I don't know a parent who can look back and say with absolutely certainty, "I did everything just right in raising my children."

What you can know as a Christian parent is that—as you love the Lord and seek to follow His direction—He promises to be with you . . . to work through you . . . and to cause all things to work together for good (even your mistakes, failures, and oversights). The Lord promises to compensate for your shortcomings, to fill in the blanks that you might have omitted.

Having this knowledge shouldn't lessen your resolve to do your utmost as a parent. It should, however, lessen your frustration and worry about your every move and action.

If you feel you have failed the Lord in your responsibility as a parent, admit that to Him and ask His forgiveness. Ask Him to reveal to you what you can and should do as a next step.

Whatever you do, don't wallow in a sense of failed parenthood. That's a condemnation trick of the devil.

If your children bring up something from the past and count it as a parental failure, weigh what they have to say. If you believe there's some merit in the accusation, repent of that failure to your children and to the Lord, and ask forgiveness. Let your children know that you did not err willfully. Reaffirm your love to them.

Even if you feel your children unjustly accuse you, the wisest course may be to say, "That may be true. I realize it's the way you see the past, and I'm sorry that you are feeling pain about this. Please forgive me. I did not take that action to cause you pain. I did not knowingly and willfully hurt you. What can I do to make it right? I love you, and I never want to do anything to damage a loving and healthy relationship between you and the Lord Jesus."

Your Children Can Never Completely Walk Away from the Faith of Your Home

When I first heard the call of God on my life to enter the ministry, I was in Switzerland. I was only fifteen years old at the time, but I came home knowing that the call of God was real. It was awesome to me, and I didn't doubt it a bit. I also didn't rejoice over it. My immediate and overwhelming reaction was one of fear.

That particular fear was definitely not of God, but I allowed it to overtake my faith and I entered into a period of rebellion—not against my parents or against Jesus but against the Lord's *demand* on my life.

I had watched my parents go through extreme difficulties during a four-year period in their ministry—a time when it seemed that every demonic onslaught possible had been thrown at them to keep them from launching a new ministry outreach. I had seen all of the behind-the-scenes work in the ministry. I knew the heartache my parents had felt over souls that had drifted from the Lord, over worthy projects that had gone underfunded, over friends who had betrayed them. Just about the last thing I wanted to do in my own life was to enter full-time ministry.

At the same time, I could not escape the reality of my parents' relationship with Jesus and the Spirit of God, who had been a very real presence to me all of my life. Within a very short time, I came to my senses and dedicated my full effort to preparing for the ministry.

I have a strong belief that my experience, though not the blatant rebellion exhibited by some, is not atypical. I also believe that children can never completely walk away from the spiritual experience seeded into their lives by godly parents.

How many adults have you heard about who came to the Lord and said as part of their testimony, "I remember how Grandma used to pray for me," or "I finally realized that what my parents had taught me all those years was really true"?

Let me call your attention to Deuteronomy 6:20–25:

When your son asks you in time to come, saying, "What is the meaning of the testimonies, the statutes, and the judgments which the LORD our God has commanded you?" then you shall say to your son: "We were slaves of Pharaoh in Egypt, and the LORD brought us out of Egypt with a mighty hand; and the LORD showed signs and wonders before our eyes, great and severe, against Egypt, Pharaoh, and all his household. Then He brought us out from there, that He might bring us in, to give us the land of which He swore to our fathers. And the LORD commanded us to observe all these statutes, to fear the LORD our God, for our good always, that He might preserve us alive, as it is this day. Then it will be righteousness for us, if we are careful to observe all these commandments before the LORD our God, as He has commanded us."

These words are directed to the children who didn't experience the original Passover. This passage anticipates the day when rituals are being kept that are not readily understood by the children—a day when Jewish children a generation removed from the deliverance from Egypt will ask, "Why are we killing a lamb this spring and keeping a Passover meal?"

I am 100 percent convinced that if children are raised by faith-filled parents and they rebel against the teachings of those parents, the day will come when the children must again confront the steadfastness of their parents in serving the Lord. The parents' example before them, from their childhood through their adulthood, will continue to influence them in a convicting way.

The Holy Spirit will not let the children get away from memories of the spiritual experiences they once enjoyed in the parents' presence. And the day will come when the rebellious children return to the parents—either face-to-face or in their inner thought life—and ask, "Why did you do what you did? What did it all mean to you?"

The testimony of the parents back to the children is a simple one with three main points. We have done what we have done and we have lived the Christian life we have lived because

• first, we were the slaves of sin, and God delivered us. He revealed His great power and love to us, and He brought us out of sin and put us into His land.

• second, the Lord our God commanded us to keep these testimonies, statutes, and judgments. We were and are obedient to Him, our Savior and Deliverer.

• third, we believe with all of our hearts that the Lord's commandments are *for our good always, that He might preserve us alive, as it is this day*. We believe God requires only things of us that are for our benefit, both now and forever. We believe that when we follow God's commandments, He preserves us and gives us an abundant life. There's a reward in serving God and keeping His law, and that reward is righteousness, or being in right standing with Him.

In other words, the parents of the rebellious children live out a witness that says, "We belong to God. We serve Him and love Him because He first loved us, and out of that love, He has asked us to keep certain commandments that are for our benefit, for the preservation and abundance of our lives."

In looking back, we may realize that we have never shared with the children the before-and-after story of our lives. Perhaps the most powerful word we can speak about the Lord Jesus is our personal testimony: "My life was like this. . . . And then Jesus met me in this way. . . . And I responded to Him like this. . . . And this is what happened in my life. . . ."

In those instances where the parent comes to know the Lord after the children are grown, the sharing of a before-and-after testimony is especially important because the children usually remember aspects of childhood that are painful because they reflected unrighteousness. Blessed is the parent who will say, "Do you remember how life was . . . that year I almost left your mother (or father) . . . the way I used to strike out at you and others in anger . . . the terrible difficulty we had with finances . . . the deep depression I sometimes felt? Let me tell you how different my life is now. . . ."

Friend, that's a difficult witness for even the most rebellious children to deny, overlook, or dismiss without a very serious evaluation.

God Isn't Through Writing Your Story

I draw great encouragement from the fact that the Bible unfolds information—line upon line, precept upon precept—in a progressive manner.

Not only has God revealed Himself in a progressive way from generation to generation, but He reveals Himself to us in the same way. We can operate only in the truth that we have now. Even so, we face a tremendous responsibility before God for doing what we know to do.

I readily admit to you that I don't know everything there is about the Word of God on passing your faith to the next generation, but I do know enough to keep me fully occupied and acutely aware of the way I'm raising my own children, 60 minutes every hour, 24 hours a day, 365 days a year.

Expect the Lord's guidance to you to be one of continuing insight, unfolding revelation, revealed direction.

Experience— and Beyond Experience

Throughout this book, I've emphasized the importance of our children having an experience with the Lord. This experience is rooted in an ongoing, daily, life-walk relationship with Him.

Even as we expect that relationship to unfold in our children's lives and, indeed, encourage that relationship, we should also let our children in on one of the great secrets about *all* relationships: They fluctuate in intensity.

At times we feel very close to another person or to the Lord. At other times we may feel less close. The reality of the relationship remains, however. That is especially so with the Lord.

He is the constant in our relationship with Him. He remains the same toward us, no matter what we do. We are the ones who move closer to or farther away from the Lord through our actions and our decisions.

"We walk by faith, not by sight" is the way the apostle Paul taught the Corinthians (2 Cor. 5:7).

Our faith tells us that God is, God loves us, God forgives us when we repent of our sins, and God is working all things to our good—regardless of how we feel at any one point in time.

Teenagers especially sometimes feel as if they are on an emotional roller coaster. With hormones that are sometimes on a roller coaster, how could their feelings be any other way? Assure your teenagers that human feelings rise and fall. The Lord's relationship with them, however, is marked by the words *steadfast, trustworthy,* and *faithful.*

One of my favorite verses in the Bible is the promise of the Lord given in 1 Thessalonians 5:24: "He who calls you is faithful, who also will do it."

Trust the Lord to bring to reality the revelation He has given you for your family. I stand with you in believing that He *will* bring to pass a fruitful faith in your life and the lives of *all* your children!

12

How Will You Choose?

Choose for yourselves this day whom you will serve.

—Joshua 24:15

When we look at the world today, one conclusion we must draw is that we live in a society in moral decay. Most teenagers do *not* have a strong ethical code by which to live.

Recently, I was ministering in a church, and my wife was helping to set up the book table in the foyer. She was approached by a vivacious five-year-old girl who spotted our tape on Teenage Mutant Ninja Turtles and proudly said, "I know them!" She then proceeded to sing, without an error, the complete opening theme song to the Teenage Mutant Ninja Turtles cartoon show.

My wife asked her, "Honey, will you sing a song for me about Jesus instead?"

The little girl responded, "I don't know any songs about Jesus."

My wife asked, "You don't know *any* songs about Jesus?" She thought perhaps it might be the little girl's first time at the church.

The little girl replied, "Oh, I know 'Jesus Loves Me' and 'Deep and Wide,' but I'd really rather sing the Turtle song." (It turned out, by the way, that the little girl was the pastor's daughter.)

My question to you today is . . .

Which song would *your* children rather sing? Which song are you training your children to sing?

It comes down to choice, doesn't it?

Choices made for ourselves.

For our children.

Before God.

Forever.

Bringing your children to a faith in God requires an *active choice.*

In Joshua's final address to the children of Israel, with whom he had wandered in the wilderness and whom he had led in the conquest of the Promised Land, he said,

> " 'I have given you a land for which you did not labor, and cities which you did not build, and you dwell in them; you eat of the vineyards and olive groves which you did not plant.'

> "Now therefore, fear the Lord, serve Him in sincerity and in truth, and put away the gods which your fathers served on the other side of the River and in Egypt. Serve the Lord! And if it seems evil to you to serve the Lord, choose for yourselves this day whom you will serve, whether the gods which your fathers served that were on the other side of the River, or the gods of the Amorites, in whose land you dwell. But as for me and my house, we will serve the Lord."

> So the people answered and said: "Far be it from us that we should forsake the Lord to serve other gods" (Josh. 24:13–16).

May each of us as Christian parents give voice to the proclamation of Joshua today: "As for me and my house, we will serve the Lord."

May we respond as the people did, saying, "Far be it

from us that we should forsake the Lord to serve other gods."

May it be far from us to forsake the Lord and the salvation of our households to serve mammon, or to pursue riches.

May it be far from us to forsake the Lord and the salvation of our children to serve our culture.

May it be far from us to forsake the Lord and the spiritual nourishment of our children to serve our own desires for prestige and status.

My Closing
Prayer with You

Father, we don't deserve all that You have done for us. We didn't deserve the death of Your Son on the cross. We didn't deserve Your grace, Your righteousness, Your renewal of us as new creations. We recognize that You gave us Your love not because we deserved Your love but because You are our heavenly Father. We are Your children, and we thank You today for making us Your children.

We thank You, too, for giving us our earthly children. Help us to see our children the way You see them. Help us to lead our children into the fullness of Your kingdom. Help us to minister to our children as You minister to them and to touch them as You touch them.

We don't want to enter eternity without our children. We don't want our children to miss out on the privilege of serving You and having an intimate fellowship with You all the days of their lives. We don't want our children to go through life without experiencing Your anointing on their lives.

Help us as parents to live our lives as exemplary in the kingdom. Don't let our homes be the gateway to sin. Let them be a refuge here on this earth and a gateway to Your presence in eternity. Help us to be hearers of Your Word and then doers of Your Word. What You have spoken to our hearts, help us to implement in our homes.

I pray this in the name of Jesus.

Amen!

 PARENT'S PLEDGE

As your parent,

I make a pledge to you today that spiritual
growth and development are the top priorities of my
life. Nothing matters to me as much as seeing
you grow up loving and serving our Lord Jesus
Christ
every day of your life.

I make a pledge to you today to walk with you on
the Way that He has set before us until the day
comes when you choose to walk that Way on your
own.

I pledge to teach you what I know to be His
truth and to share with you my own relationship
with our heavenly Father. My prayer and hope are
that you might always sense His presence and know
without a shadow of a doubt that you are loved
eternally and without measure by the Lord God
almighty.

I pledge to intercede before the Lord on your
behalf frequently and with all my heart that you
might come to accept Jesus Christ as your personal
Savior and Lord and to know Him as your Friend
forever.

You are my beloved child,

_____

(child's name)

and my greatest desire is to live in heaven with
you and our Lord Jesus Christ for all of
eternity.

_____   _____

(parent's name)   *(date)*